OH, LORDS!

CH. LOPESS

OH, LORDS!

Who We Date, Why We Date Them, and What We've Learned

JES AVERHART &
TERRESA ZIMMERMAN

STONEBROOK
PUBLISHING

Stonebrook Publishing
Saint Louis, Missouri

A STONEBROOK PUBLISHING BOOK

Library of Congress Control Number: 2021911372

Paperback ISBN: 978-1-955711-03-6
eBook ISBN: 978-1-955711-04-3

www.stonebrookpublishing.net
PRINTED IN THE UNITED STATES OF AMERICA

DEDICATION

To those who inspired it.
If you're wondering whether or not I'm writing
about you . . . probably.
~Jes

If changing a single thing means I wouldn't be right here right
now, I wouldn't. David, while it took too long, we got it right.
~Terresa

CONTENTS

PREFACE

 One evening, not that long ago, we met up at a local microbrewery to catch up. That "Hey girl, heeeey" moment led to Jes sharing a lighthearted story about an upcoming first date. She met this guy in seat 17C on a plane the week before while flying from New York to Durham. The next morning, she was headed back to the Big Apple on business, and she and seat 17C were planning to meet for drinks.

I'll let her tell it...

 Ha, Terresa, I remember that evening at the brewery well. 17C was a cool guy with a dry sense of humor. I didn't want to talk to him that day on the plane, which was evident because I had my earphones in, but he was smart, funny, and determined—so conversation ensued. I learned quite a bit about him, that he came from a privileged background and was (ehhh-hmmm) fourteen years younger than me. He learned that I was aloof, dated exclusively "out of market," and really didn't like to be bothered. This was his cue to throw his own earphones in and accept defeat, but he didn't. He held his own, and we exchanged numbers before grabbing our carry-ons from the overhead compartment.

Now, as I remember, I told this story to you and the group while I was drinking a beer named: *I Don't Know If You Know This, But I'm Kind of a Savage* (the irony) and asked, "Do I have drinks with him?" "Should I tell him my age?" "Is this an actual date anyway?"

This story opened the floodgates that led to more storytelling, laughter, and the time when Terresa successfully hired a dating agent.

Ah, yes, the dating agent. Here's the thing, I had ten years of being single between my practice marriage and the marriage I got right. I had lots of fun but wasn't finding the life partner I wanted. So, after a night celebrating my birthday, I decided, in my drunken brilliance, that I couldn't keep doing the same things, dating the same guys/types of guys, and expect a different outcome. So, in my state of inebriation, I left a classy message for a dating agency.

When they called me back, I had to act like I knew who they were and why they were returning my call. Doh! A dating agent was my idea of a personal shopper . . . for men. I signed up. What did I have to lose? Nothing, yet everything to gain. Even if I didn't meet someone, I'd have a great time. Meet new people. I'd take notes. I'd write a book . . .

Amidst the laughter and advice-giving that evening, we shared more stories and joked about writing it all down. Best seller in the making. Yadda. Yadda. After the tab was paid and the night was over, we decided to hold each other to it and write this book.

> *What we will tell you all along this journey is that you are in control of your dating experience, and intention is a good thing, even a must!*

Oh, Lords! is a book of dating warnings, dating glories, and dating stories—and boy, do we have stories!

This is not a how-to book. We aren't going to evaluate the best dating apps. We won't tell you the ins and outs or pros and cons of online dating versus spotting the love of your life while swingin' a kettlebell at the gym. Nope, our message begins after the connection has been made, and you're meeting across the table on the first date, in the bed after a one-nighter, or on the couch of the heartbreak. We unmask the Lords you'll likely encounter along the way, share our experiences, and let you in on what we learned with each. What we *will* tell you all along this journey is that *you* are in control of your dating experience, and intention is a good thing, even a must!

Before you dive in, there are a few things you should know about us. We are wicked smart women. Intelligent. Discerning. Ambitious. We're leaders, successful in many realms, and *fun!* Okay, fine, yes, we're adorable, and we have hilariously similar dating stories with spookily similar lessons.

But here's the deal: we date men. We've written our stories from our heterosexual perspectives (although Jes has experimented along the way). And just because you may have different identifi-cations and preferences, don't think you get to escape any of the follies and foibles contained in this book. No way, no how! We all have dating drama. We encourage you to change those pronouns if you need to and then lean in.

Oh, Lords! can be read as gender agnostic. You're going to recognize these archetypes even if you do change the pronouns because women and men can both fall into our Lord archetypes. This is a fully inclusive human condition.

The Dating Landscape

Let's start with a dating level-set. According to a 2021 report issued by The Business of Apps, the global revenue share for dating apps at the end of 2020 was $3.08 billion, powered primarily by Tinder and Bumble. With that in mind, it's no surprise that more than 25 percent of US couples meet online. Other sites like Match, Hinge, OkCupid, eharmony, and even Grindr rule the day. As we write this, 44 percent of the American population is single, and forty million of them are using online dating services. Makes sense, right? Technology has made it easier than ever to promote yourself, screen potential dates, and connect with hopeful matches. Clearly, the business of dating is booming—and the mystery of dating is still ever-present.

Tinder offers the sequencing of dating through their "12 Stages of Sex and Dating" philosophy. We've always been inclined to com-pare the emotional journey of dating to a twelve-step program, so we're glad Tinder agrees. Let's learn how they define these stages (with a little extra help from us).

Stage 1 - Going into the First Date
This is the stage where the pressure is on. It's time to summon your alter ego and go for it. (Jes calls on "Cinnamon Sassafrass" during these times.)

Stage 2 - After the First Date
In this stage, you might feel like you're in suspended animation. *Uh, now what? Do we do this again? Who asks who out?*

Stage 3 - The First Kiss
This is where we disagree with the Tinder experts. We know that the kiss is probably happening before the second date. But either way, you're stepping on the emotional bridge. You're physically connecting for the first time. Now, the real tests begin.

Stage 4 - The First Time You Have Sex
The emotional bridge has now been crossed. Good or bad, sex takes the connection deeper.

Stage 5 - Having Sex More Regularly
So . . . if you're having it more regularly, we hope the sex was good. At this point, one or both parties are likely "catching feelings."

Stage 6 - Dating Casually
This is the one-foot-in, one-foot-out stage. It's also where you start to drop the alter ego. Bye, bye Cinnamon Sassafras!

Stage 7 - Fizzling Out
Now, the tension of your time versus your emotional investment comes into play. It's the "So we doing this? Or nah?" moment.

Stage 8 - Opening Up to Each Other
This is a good stage. It's the Brené Brown Stage. Time to be vulnerable, be your authentic self, and keep it all the way real!

Stage 9 - Hanging Out with Each Other's Friends
Mm, the seismic size up. You might endure a swirl of old stories and third-wheel feelings while hoping to earn your wings when it's all said and done. They like you . . . they *really like you*!

Stage 10 - Saying "I Love You"
Ahh, the shot heard 'round the world. When this moment happens, we tell our friends how it went down, who said it first, how fast the other person said it back—or if they said it at all. This moment sets the stage for #11 and #12.

Stage 11 - Becoming Exclusive
You're off the dating market. How's that workin' for you? Time to evaluate if this is the move—long term.

Stage 12 - Slapping a Label on It
This stage might happen at the same time as #11, but oftentimes, it's separate. After a period of moving with exclusivity, you then step all the way into "Look at us, we're a couple" mode. This is when it becomes official and verbal. You're hitching your wagon to each other for the rest of the world to see.

If you're like us, you related to all these stages, but it's also not as neat and tidy as that. Sequential order is great. Stages are great. But not all of us want to go through all of them—and not sequentially. We want to spend a lot of time on some of them. We're quite happy to skip a few of them. Random order may even be fun!

In the next several pages, you're going to hear our stories. And they don't always follow the rules above. But as we tell them, there's a 100 percent chance that you'll start telling your own. It's true: we can be "judgey" in our tellings, and we do label people. (We call them archetypes.) But we're painfully honest. Very real. We've had to say stuff out loud that we're not very proud of. Oh boy, we would rather deny a few things, but we don't. We own it, and we want you to know it. Along with having some fun, maybe you can relate, and just maybe, you can even use our experiences to avoid some of our mistakes.

The Lords

And now for our "Lords." These guys will feel familiar to you. You've dated them. Broken up with them. Married them. In all of those cases, they left an indelible impression—for better or worse. We'll share our stories of love and loss and bring these Lords to life, so you can recognize them in your dating journey. For these reasons and more, let's meet the Lords.

- Lord Journeyman—easy and conventional
- Lord Contradiction—says one thing, goes after another
- Lord FOMO—grass is always greener
- Lord Layaway—playa, playa
- Lord Self-Absorbed—me, myself, and I
- Lord At-Your-Peril—abusive—bad news bear
- Lord Good Guy, Not My Guy—self-explanatory
- Lord My Guy—the one

Like we said, in the following chapters, we'll share what we've learned, and you'll notice that sometimes we were slow learners. And while it wasn't always funny, we've had to laugh at ourselves! Please, laugh with us—or at us—too.

But first, you need to know us.

JES

Before we dive into the dating drama, I want you to know me, so let's start with my dating journey.

Who Am I?

 How did I get to this point? Well, it takes a village. Or rather, it took a village to raise me. I grew up in the tiny, unincorporated village of Evansport, Ohio. A dot on the map that had a population of about 284 people living within its borders, 99 percent of whom were white. My blackness made up part of the 1 percent. Being the only African American in a small, Midwestern, white community in the eighties and nineties might seem like it was fraught with challenges, but it was quite the contrary.

Let me explain my family. My grandparents were upper-middle class. They built very successful businesses from scratch. They were scrappy, and it paid off. My family owned the local insurance agency, the skating rink, an auction house, and a real estate appraisal and brokerage firm. Because they were respected, I was protected and off-limits to public scorn or speculation. If people talked about my mom bringing home a Black baby from the Army, it happened quietly over their own dinner tables, period.

My mom, a petite 5'4" white woman, took me back to Evansport in 1979, when I was three. She'd been in the military for almost nine years, and I was born out of wedlock while she was stationed in Germany. My birth story is like a made-for-TV movie, and I won't unpack it all in this book. But let's just say that my mom was a badass, and she defied all 1976 logic by facing the critics and bringing her nine-pound bundle of ebony into her ivory world.

From the age of three until I turned eighteen, my world existed in Northwest Ohio, where I earned my degree in people-pleasing. It was hardwired. At the age of six, my family put me to work for the family business—the Sigg Auction company. My job required me to navigate an adult world with expertise. I carried on witty and polite adult conversations at a very young age because my grandpa had me by his side every step of the way. If he was in conversation, I was listening. The local farmers, teachers, antique collectors, and investors alike knew me by name and thought I was delightful. Turns out, these lessons would serve as a double-edged sword in my relationships down the road and would have to be carefully managed.

In high school, my senior year superlatives were Most Likely to Succeed, Outstanding High School Student, Most School Spirit, and Best Personality. I worked very hard to fit in and be liked by everyone in my class. I wanted my goth/heavy metal classmates to love me as much as the preppy athletic clique—and they did. And I loved them back; mission accomplished.

Where I always fell woefully short was in romantic relationships. I knew that at school, I would safely remain in the friend zone with all the boys. From kindergarten through high school, I was one of two Black kids in my class. I knew I didn't have a chance with the white boys. I knew my lane, and I stayed in it. Now, this little roadblock didn't mean I didn't have crushes, oh, did I have crushes! But they were always squashed when I inevitably had to help one of my girl-friends figure out if *my* crush liked *her*! Check: Yes or No (eye roll).

It wasn't until my sophomore year that I kissed a boy—a real kiss. Like, he put his foreign tongue in my mouth, and I tried to match his excitement. This kid wasn't from my school. A class-mate brought him along to the school dance, and I was the lucky winner. All I remember is that he was older than me, wore MC Hammer pants, and thought I was cute enough or naive enough to kiss him that night. I remember thinking, *Cool! I'm moving up in the world. I don't have to lie about being kissed anymore.* Mission accomplished.

Ah, spring of 1993, the year I got my driver's license. Now listen, when you're from a rural community, you don't really start living until you have your driver's license! I got mine, and I was bee-bopping to Nichole and Stacy's houses, parked in the Burger King parking lot after the games, and running to the mall at will. I finally had carte blanche of my life and could live it with a measured touch of reckless abandon.

It was on one of these great escapes that I met Kendrick. He was a boy from a neighboring school who I'd met after a football game—did I mention I was a cheerleader? Yeah, so I was a Black cheerleader—in a white school—with a driver's license. Watch out, brothas, I was making up for lost time! Anyway, I lost my mind over Kendrick. He was *fine*, like cover-of-a-magazine fine, with strong cheekbones, a square chin, kind eyes, and a smile that lit up a room. Apparently, he was diggin' on me too because, after a few phone calls and another planned meetup after one of my football games, he asked me to be his homecoming date. Finally, in the fall of my senior year, I was going to be someone's date.

Honestly, I don't remember it. I literally don't remember Homecoming! I don't remember the theme or the dancing. I know it happened because I have a picture of it somewhere. But what I do remember is riding back in his car with my head on his lap, saying, "You can't take me home yet."

During that car ride, I decided that I would not be the only virgin in homeroom. So, while poor Kendrick was unprepared and overwhelmed, he played the *Rocky* soundtrack in his mind and manned up. He took me back to his place and . . . mission accomplished.

I didn't love him, but I tried to. Sadly, two things happened that prevented a more torrid love affair from unfolding. (1) He had a manipulative side and would get handsy and forceful with me if he wasn't getting his way. Fortunately, this never became physical abuse, but it got too close for comfort once, and I'd had enough. (2) He went to jail not long after this incident for grand theft auto and possession of a firearm. So yeah, that'll end a relationship.

First Love

The first boy I loved was Ty. He was from Defiance, about fifteen miles from Evansport. I knew him because he was an athlete and ran in the crew that every girl wanted to associate with. Ty and I had only spoken in passing. Then in late winter of my senior year, I saw him at the mall. We talked, we flirted, and we exchanged numbers. He called.

Ty was a gentleman. We talked for hours, we went on dates, we dreamed about our future together, and he helped me navigate the loss of my grandfather. We also had a lot of sex. Like under trees, in my car, in his car, on friends' couches—everywhere. I loved him for real, and at a time when I was vulnerable and needed some assurances in life, he was like water in a desert.

Then he joined the Army.

In the fall of 1994, I headed to college, and he was off to basic training. We did what all young love does—we said we'd stay together, that we were strong enough and nothing could separate us. By Christmas of that year, it was over. It turns out the distance was too vast, and our love wasn't strong enough to blind me from my future husband.

My Real Love

I met Marc my freshman year at Ohio Northern University. Go Polar Bears! He walked into the cafeteria after football practice with his greys on. That's what the girls called the standard-issue grey football sweats that the players wore. Ooooh weee, the sweatsuit greys were *sexy*, and he wore them well.

For the sake of this story, let me summarize our young love. We met when I was eighteen, and we broke up once or twice along the way. But we always made up and were inseparable and happy for many, many years. We were in love, but it was more than that. We were best friends. He was my ride or die. Marc and I got engaged over Christmas my senior year in college. We graduated, moved to Cincinnati, and got married three months later. Yep, it was a whirlwind, but it was right.

Four years later, we had our son. Having Tre seemed to bring it all together for us. We had a model marriage and were on our way to having a model family. Then we weren't.

The truth is, *marriage is hard,* people! Getting married at twenty-two is even harder, and being married at twenty-two amidst a changing and connected world is reserved for champions. I thought I was a champion—that we were champions—and it turns out that our fatal flaws still found us.

Looking back on my marriage, I was in love, yes, but I was also playing a role. Although I was raised by a single mom, I knew what the role of a conventional wife looked like, so I put on that costume each day. In hindsight, I see that our perfect little marriage had tiny cracks that eventually gave way. I was personally and professionally unfulfilled, and I wandered. I needed more. I needed some risk and reward, and ultimately, I probably just needed to invest more time in learning who I was instead of trying to perfect my part. Duality can wreak havoc in your life; it did in our marriage.

The End I The Beginning

It wasn't fair for me to stay in a relationship that no longer fit, and I didn't want to put on the costume of a woman I no longer wanted to be. Some people ask what happens to the fairy tale after *I do?* In our case, we did live happily ever after—just apart. Marc was exactly who he said he was and still is. He's amazing, we're friends, and we've successfully co-parented an incredible young man (nay-sayers be damned!).

Since then, I've been happily single. I date openly and have for a few years. For me, this means I almost always date "out of market"—mainly in other states—because it's most conducive to how I move.

Ask my girlfriends. They'll tell you that I refer to each man with a geographic term of endearment. There's Birmingham Boo, Oakland Boo, DC Boo, Miami Boo, Atlanta Boo, another DC Boo, and a Manhattan Boo. I didn't date all of these men at the same time, but a few overlapped, and that was sort of the point—the freedom to date and explore!

I get that my dating philosophy is unique and earns a few side-eyes. When you dive into this book, you'll see that I'm the Lady equivalent to Lord FOMO, and we are a rare sort. Sure, I've dated exclusively. I have commitment in me; I was married for twelve years, for heaven's sake, but much of that was guided by convention and timing.

Like a lot of women, I've played the damsel in distress countless times and even remained celibate for a season to wait for "the One." Dating is like dieting; I've tried it all, and these days, I've given up impulsive and random dating in favor of logic and convenience. I know this might appear cold and businesslike, and you're probably asking yourself, *Where's the romance? Where's the spontaneity? Where's the LOVE, Jes?!* I know, I know, but right now, this is what works for me.

2

TERRESA

 My turn. Guess what? I'm married—very happily. It's my second attempt. When I was dating between marriages, unlike Jes, I always wanted to find a life partner, someone to share life and experiences with, someone to grow with. This was fundamental to my approach to dating.

I met my amazing husband through a dating agent. When she called to arrange our first meeting, she described a tall, dark, handsome, professional, educated, fun health nut. Since I lived in San Francisco, the *health nut* part had me a little worried. It conjured up images of any number of don't-believe-in-deodorant, will-strap-myself-to-a-trunk-to-save-a-tree, gluten-free, vegan, carb-free, dieting kind of health nut. David is the Texas kind that believes mac and cheese is a vegetable, and a health nut meant a gym rat. Happy all around.

We both told our dating agent that we needed someone who could keep up with us and even challenge us. Using nearly the exact same terms with her, we described what we wanted in a partner. We wanted to be pushed constructively. We wanted to grow with someone. We wanted to lead our lives with possibility and know our partner was right there thinking of even more possibilities.

It's so easy to hold someone back in a relationship. Been with those guys. No thank you. It's hard to help someone be more, do more, grow more. David does that for me. And I do that for him. It's our natural inclination, but it's also a very conscious intent in the way we live and the way we interact and react with each other in daily life.

Neither of us came to this position easily. Lots of trials and even more errors. You'll hear many of those in this book. And maybe we came to it by experiencing all that we didn't want, but I think we're both naturally grounded in growth, improvement, and possibility. And that fundamental need, value, belief, perspective—whatever word you choose—to grow and be challenged is definitively us. It defines us every day.

Who Am I?

It was a long road to get here. I was born on an army base in Arizona, and I grew up in Utah as a Mormon. Not necessarily the "going to church every week as a family" kind, but Mormon enough. My friends and their families were all Mormon. All our activities seemed to involve the church and its gyms and fields and halls, at least until halfway through eighth grade when we moved to California after my parents' divorce. After that, I was pretty much on my own. I sought religious education for myself from about eight different groups, including Mormons. But I decided organized religion wasn't at all my thing.

I was also on my own in other ways. I took care of things. I cleaned the house. I cooked dinner. I took care of myself. I took care of my two younger brothers, too, the youngest being ten years my junior. I was not interested in my parents, and frankly, I was angry at my dad for "abandoning" us. (We have a great relationship now, btw.)

I had no use for my mother, and she wasn't interested in me either. She was working. She was finding herself. Did I mention that she married my dad when she was only seventeen? What? Of course, she had to find herself! Then she started dating. Oh boy. She has dating stories too. I made sure to get her inside and shut the door on more than one of her dates. (Sorry, Mom. NOT.) When I got to high school, I paid less attention to my brothers but still tried to take care of things while moving on with my life. I had boxes to check and things to accomplish. I wanted more out of life than I even knew existed. I had a belief it was all out there, and I needed to *go get it.*

Looking Back

We didn't have a lot of stuff growing up. I wore my dad's boss's grandson's throwaway jeans (which I loved—thank you!), but we had what we needed, and I knew I was secure. I knew I could do anything I set my mind to. I knew I was capable. I knew that I could make it all happen, whatever *it* was.

I remember a direct conversation with my dad around fourth grade when he said, "You can be anything you want to be, even

President." Maybe that's a generational thing, being told that you can be President of the United States. But I got the message. There was nothing I couldn't do with enough work and focus and faith.

So, why is this important for a book about dating lessons? Because my belief that my life was up to me and my internal security is my foundation. Even in all the moments that I felt like a misfit—like I never belonged anywhere—I always believed that I had control of myself and where I could go. For the good and the bad of it, it led me to a *What's the worst that can happen? I'll be able to figure it out, jump then think* approach to life—and men.

First Love

I met my first longish-term boyfriend in high school. He was quintessential, captain and quarterback of the football team, student body president, cute, popular, and well-liked. He checked all those glamour boxes. He was a senior. I was a sophomore. While I felt like an awkward nobody, he chose me.

Then he graduated, and I set my sights on high school accomplishments and my life plan. Student body president. Check that box. Outstanding senior girl. Check. Got into all the universities where I applied. Check. Check. Check. And all the way along, he was jealous, controlling, and protective. You know that guy who flexes his muscles and holds you that much tighter when another guy walks past? That was him. Making his statement. I didn't like it. But I guess I thought that was love.

I remember when a rival school's team bus was in our school parking lot, and one of the guys decided to moon us all—as you do at that age. My boyfriend was furious at the injustice that I, *his* girlfriend, would have to see that nakedness through a dirty window. Fights were threatened. Did he think I'd be flattered? Really? It was funny. I was confused by his behavior. His girlfriend sees a naked butt—that's going to set off a brawl? Juvenile.

I wasn't impressed, but that didn't break us up. He wanted all my time, so I was *that girl* who dropped all my girlfriends for my boyfriend but not fully because I was still at school without him for nearly two years. But it did mean I kept a certain emotional and physical distance from my peers.

He was my first. No doubt, being occupied with and by him for nearly all three years of high school kept me out of all kinds of teen-age trouble. He wanted to keep me in a box. A box with him, but still a box. He had a ton going for him in high school. That was very attractive. But that's where it ended. I outgrew him. He was more interested in planning my life than his. In fairness, he didn't know what he wanted to do, but none of us do at that age, even if some of us are more confident in publicly claiming we do. He's probably the same guy now, which is totally fine. For him.

The Boyfriend Loop

At the last minute, I ended up at the University of Colorado Boulder, where I played a lot, skied a bunch, and went to school enough to get the grades to transfer to Santa Clara University. College was a checkbox for me. I wanted to do whatever was necessary to finish and move on, so I could start my life.

I had a ton of fun in college—so much fun that let's just say that even without a social media timeline, I'll never be able to run for any public office. I dated *a lot*. I could not be serious with anyone, and even though I think I was clear about not wanting to be settled and serious, I left a wake. I always wanted a relationship, but later. That was not a box to be checked yet. That was for after graduation, and it needed to be with someone who was already doing something. Being someone. I was definitely not the kind of girl that a mom would want her more serious-about a-relationship son to date. I was playing the field.

Plus, I always had a certain person in the background—for nearly twenty years! You'll hear more about him later, but this guy was my long-term sweetheart and fallback guy, meaning whenever I wasn't dating someone, I always reached back out to him, regardless of where I was in the world. And he always responded.

Practice Marriage

Cycle forward: I jumped into a marriage with an American man I met when I was living in Japan, working for a Japanese company, speaking grocery-store Japanese, with no local friends; I was seriously isolated. He was funny and popular and ran with a crowd. But he was not a good person. And he didn't bring out anything good in me. So crazy because he was funny and popular, right? Everyone wanted to be around him. What could possibly go wrong? Stay tuned for Lord At-Your-Peril.

The simple truth is that no one knows what goes on behind closed doors. My marriage was short but impactful. He was attracted to me because I was strong and ambitious. And those were exactly the traits he actively sought to control and cancel in me. I'd never run into that before. I didn't know what to do with it. I wasn't looking after myself in that relationship. No good comes from that. Divorce was my reawakening. I started to truly know myself then. And life started getting so much better.

These three relationships were pivotal for me, and they set the tone for my personal journey. If you think about your foundations as your frame of reference—your guide—you can look at your experiences as the application or testing of those foundations. My foundations—the values I grew up with—proved they weren't foolproof. They didn't give me a roadmap to my journey. But they are the platform from which I could experiment. Have successes. Make mistakes. Recover. Feel confident. Discover and test insecurities. And ultimately, seek out the life I want and those whom I choose to share it with, and the journey—the experiment—continues. Lots of trials. A ton of errors. Amazing experiences. And an even greater hold on leading my life with positivity and possibility.

Now, it's time to meet our first Lord.

3

LORD JOURNEYMAN

"This is not that hard! Where the fuck are we going this weekend? Are we going to go the country, the beach, or the mountains—the beach or the mountains?"

"I'll get back to you on Thursday."

"Never mind."

jour·ney·man

/ˈjərnēmən/

noun

1. a worker or sports player who is competent and reliable but not outstanding.

L ord Journeyman is a good guy. Responsible. Predictable. Steady. Planned. He's a great catch—everyone thinks so. This Lord is the accountant, the engineer, the rock. The one who will always be there.

When you're with Lord Journeyman, things, within reason, will be planned—well in advance. This Lord loves routine, and it's hard for him to do anything that's not part of the plan or already part of his world. Really hard. But Lord Journeyman has a lot of great qualities and can be tons of fun. And above all else, this Lord is *there.* Always there.

That's Lord Journeyman.

I met Lord Journeyman on a cruise at the end of high school. He was tall, dark, handsome, and several years older. Funny. Gentle. He had friends and a social group that positively glittered. He loved to go out and have fun. Dance, dance, dance. He and his friends had a couple of group dance routines they did in clubs where they took over the dance floor and the entire scene. I'm sure it was part of their pickup tricks. And it worked. He was a blast. I was in love.

Over the next twenty years, our relationship was mostly long distance. I'd be between international moves or boyfriends or what-ever, and I'd reconnect with my Lord Journeyman. I'd fly through the airport in his city, and he'd always be there to meet me for a quick catch-up, maybe a quickie, and sometimes, there was a short-lived rekindling of our romance. I did a lot of growing up while he was in my life, so he got to see A LOT of my growing pains; of college life, freshman fifteen, clubbing/drinking downsides (throwing up in his mother's roses!), hair color experimentation, girl drama, and more. Whatever it was, he took it all in stride and made me feel like it was all normal and a part of life. He didn't judge me. Being with him was like lounging in my sweats and socks—cozy, comfortable, nestled—oh, and super-sexy.

He was my background guy, my fallback guy. I just needed to go out and live a little, and afterward, I thought, Lord Journeyman would be *the one* for me. After college, I moved to Japan. I asked him to come with me. He didn't. I asked him to give me that year away, and then I'd come back to us. He said "no," probably rightly so. He was like a grounding wire that would always tug and pull me back after any and all the crazy, adventurous stuff I thought I needed to get out of my system.

I always thought I'd go back to him at some point when the time was right, when I was ready to settle down and be there for him. *He's amazing*, I thought. *He's my guy. But I need to go do these other things before I can come back and be the right person for him.* He wasn't asking me to do that. He would never have asked that of me. I knew I'd have to be a different person, a more settled person, in order to have him. In fact, he once asked if I thought we'd be married with six kids if I hadn't moved overseas after college. I think I said "sure." Ahem. That was never in my plan.

Here's the thing: *It was always me going back to him.* We had a lot of big gaps during those twenty years, and we were never exclusive. I didn't ever think very hard about the fact that I was always molding to his way, but that ended up being our issue, both in the moment and ultimately at the end. I started to see in myself that I'm a very mobile person. I like to get up and go. I like to get up and do. At a critical moment for us, he didn't have a passport, which was disastrous to me because what it really said was, "I'm content right where I am." There is absolutely nothing wrong with that. But I wanted him to want more out of life, wanted him to do more with me, and I knew I'd become resentful.

I finally realized that you shouldn't have to *go back*, that I couldn't go back. A partner is supposed to *move forward* with you. And I would never be one to settle down and be satisfied without lots of movement.

A partner is supposed to move forward with you.

I've taken all of the personality tests—Myers Briggs, Innovation Assessment—there's a thousand of them out there. And I always test high on innovation. I have a "jump, then think" approach to life. My Lord Journeyman could never deal with that. And even if he could, it would mean I'd be going off on my own. A lot. And I'd have to be okay with that.

Ultimately, that's not what I wanted. You can't make someone want what they don't want, or be someone they aren't. At least I don't believe so.

 Well, I married Lord Journeyman. My ex was truly my sweetheart. He was all the things, and I felt like the luckiest girl on my college campus. I'd found the perfect guy. At eighteen years old, perfect meant marriage material, and he was all that. Adoring, devoted, loyal, spiritual, sensible, and loving.

Women love these Lords because they ooze stability. They are grounded in principles and immovable in many ways around traditional schools of thought. The downside, if you had to name a few, is that they often lack spontaneity, flexibility, and the ability to lean into risk.

My Lord Journeyman was also predictable, brooding, thoughtful, and conventional. But I'm not like that; I'm predisposed to experiment. My flow is, *Who knows what the hell I'll do next week or next year.* My journeyman was an engineer by trade. Security, foundation, predictability; that's his base. It was always "think a lot, and then you jump." And because, like Terresa, I'm much more "jump then think," the few conflicts we had grew into unhealthy roots that would be hard to pull out later when it counted.

It drove me crazy because he couldn't make a decision. It would take him three days to make a simple decision. I'm not kidding—three days! Three days, three whole days, to make a decision about anything other than where we would eat dinner—and he could only decide that because dinner was that day. But any major decision (and all decisions seemed major to him), like what will we do this weekend, should we go visit your parents for Thanksgiving, what day should we leave—he couldn't decide.

"This is not that hard! Where the fuck are we going this weekend? Are we going to go the country, the beach, or the mountains—the beach or the mountains?"

"I'll get back to you on Thursday."

"Never mind."

By Thursday, I didn't even want to go anywhere. Where's the spontaneity?

Decisions overwhelmed him. With Lord Journeyman, there is no jump, then think.

He's now my ex.

But he was the right guy at the right time. No one could have convinced me otherwise. He was foundational for me, a rock in many ways. No one could have told me that anyone on the planet was better suited for me than my Lord Journeyman.

He's obviously grown over the years and has evolved over time, but to the core of who he is, he's Lord Journeyman. In my experience, this Lord feels irresponsible if he veers away from the predictable. To be a little bit spontaneous or a little more off the cuff can seem reckless. And they don't like that.

Looking back, I can say with a clear conscience that my ex was my most precious love. He's the father to our son and is truly a wonderful man. I'm categorizing him as Lord Journeyman because that's how I experienced him when we met in college and through-out our marriage, but he could also be classified as "Lord Good Guy, Not MY Guy."

Because of his nature, he was patient and forgiving in a time when I made choices that ultimately destroyed our marriage. When he had every right to be cold and unabashed, he was not. During the twelve years I was married to my Lord Journeyman, I was able to fully appreciate who he was and who I was becoming, and he allowed me the space to do that.

This is a Coveted Lord

Lord Journeyman is coveted. This Lord is right for a lot of people. This Lord is Cam from *Modern Family,* Randall from *This is Us,* and

Steve from *Sex and the City*. We're like, "Right, that's the guy we're all supposed to try to find out there." And you're like, "That's my guy." He's *almost* everybody's guy.

 So many women would love to marry Jes's ex-husband, but he wasn't *her* guy because the Journeyman qualities didn't fit her. And when you're dealing with women like us, those qualities aren't helpful or inspiring. They actually create tension. When there's tension, Lord Journeymen think you don't value what they bring to the table. And that isn't good for them either.

Lessons from Lord Journeyman

Lord Journeyman, for both of us, was the right guy at the right time for a period of time. Lots of good came out of those relationships.

It takes lots of communication for women like us to date—or marry—Lord Journeyman and be successful. Both parties need to have the space to get filled up in other ways outside of the relationship. Perhaps we could have managed with our Lord Journeymen; we just needed the freedom to have more outlets, then come back to him as our home base. We clearly didn't manage it. *Could* and *should* have come into play here. You can't force fit it, even—maybe especially—for selfish reasons. We *could* manage it, but would that have been fair to our Lord Journeymen? Likely not. And at the end of the day, our Lord Journeymen were not what we needed either.

Certain Lord Journeymen traits like being predictable, committed, loyal, and adoring are super attractive, foundational traits we'd look for in any dating or life partner. But for us, it's going to be a different version of Lord. Not Lord Journeyman, but those same stellar qualities. He is, after all, a great Lord.

4

LORD CONTRADICTION

One evening, my short, blonde, non-organized-religion self was sharing a bottle of wine with this Lord on my couch in a pretty comfy position. We'd had a great evening. Fun conversation. We'd been seeing each other for a few months.

"Tell me about your ideal girlfriend or life mate," I say.

Without hesitation, he responds, "Tall, brunette, Catholic."

con·tra·dic·tion

/ˌkäntrəˈdikSH(ə)n/

noun

1. a person, thing, or situation in which inconsistent elements, denials, or opposites are present.

T his Lord can take many forms: the one who's never been married but always talks about wanting to be married; the one who says family is important yet does nothing to get there and, in fact, hates kids; the guy who dates capable, intelligent, serious women but can only fantasize about strippers and porn stars. (Sorry, ladies. We do love you.)

Lord Contradiction Type 1

Cognitive dissonance is a big term for a big concept. In this book, we call it *contradiction* for short. Contradiction in beliefs, values, and behavior. Saying or believing one thing and doing another. Normally, people strive for coherence, but when the balance between beliefs, values, and behavior gets off-kilter, it can be very uncomfortable and even damaging. Oh, *and* time- and emotion-wasting. We all experience it to some degree. Like when we know what our partner is looking for, and we then try to live up to it by changing core parts of ourselves. We may not even be aware when cognitive dissonance is present or how it shows up in our relationships, but it's there.

Most beliefs are contextual. Contradictions don't have to be intentional or deceptive. So, this Lord can get the benefit of the doubt, *a lot*. You can't simply assume he is mean-spirited. This Lord may not have a defined intention in dating. What? Are you saying Lord Contradiction may not know what he wants? Yep. And you might not either. Not everyone thinks deeply about what they want. Some just date. And, when it comes to a bird-in-the-hand date, Lord Contradiction can talk himself into a lot and find his date absolutely perfect—or at least perfect in the moment.

This is a head vs. heart contradiction. One person in the relationship always leads; one always gets ignored. You'll feel it if Lord Contradiction isn't quite there with you. You have conversations with yourself and probably your friends that go something like this:

"But he's gorgeous, sweet, smart, and funny. He's a great date; he's so thoughtful—but something's missing . . . No, never mind. He's perfect for me."

If you've had this conversation in your head, then trust your gut.

 This guy I dated had everything going for him—successful, highly intelligent, good-looking, extremely fit, not an ounce of fat, well-rounded, salt of the earth, open for anything. Fun. We started as friends, as running buddies and dates to the symphony, and it evolved from there. We kind of just fell into dating. My friend, his sister-in-law, was pushing for it and not in a subtle way. But of course! Why wouldn't we date?

"Tell me about your ideal girlfriend or life mate," I said.

Without hesitation, he responded, "Tall, brunette, Catholic."

Oh boy.

This is Lord Contradiction.

Lord Contradiction Type 2

And then there's the Lord Contradiction of a totally different style. This Lord variant knows what he wants but dates differently for other reasons. This Lord is simply dating out of convenience, dating people who aren't ideal—or even close. Women and men both do this all the time. Just look back and think about the people you've dated.

Can you see your contradictions? Some of these mismatches can be hysterical.

I have a Lord Contradiction in my history. I dated a guy while I was separated from my husband, and we fell in love pretty quickly. He was impulsive and fun; I was impulsive and liked to be talked into having fun. He was a very successful serial entrepreneur; I was a fourth-generation entrepreneur with mad drive and ambition. He was separated; I was separated. He was adventurous and a total risk-taker, and so was I. We were basically a mirror version of each other.

Now, this could be really cool. In some cases, dating your equivalent can work out. But in this case, I was with Lord Contradiction. Even though we were having a great time together, and it all seemed to click in place initially, what he really wanted and needed was a predictable, low-key partner who would cook incredible meals each night, plan trips for the family, attend church regularly on Sunday, manage the household, and not have competing and demanding professional aspirations.

It took us three months to figure this out. When we did, we broke up, and he dated and married the type of woman he really wanted, complementing his life perfectly. Meanwhile, he and I are still friends, cheering each other on in our professional pursuits and grateful that we discovered what role we were supposed to play in one another's lives.

I dated Lord Contradiction of the second variety too. This guy was a partner at a successful, big consulting firm. He had tons of friends, loved to travel, and he was active, articulate, and intelligent. This hardworking Lord and his brother also ran a family business in the South. I ended up feeling sorry for this Lord. I know none of this sounds like he needs any pity yet. But wait for it.

I met this Lord through a dating agent. Our first kiss was the worst. Seriously, maybe the worst kiss ever. I drove home thinking I must have totally blown it all out of proportion; no kiss could be that bad. It was. That was not our last date. We went on several. Kissing got more tolerable, but it didn't become a big part of our interaction. I'm still shaking my head, thinking that kissing him couldn't possibly be as bad as I remember it. Really.

Anyway, we had a lot in common. He'd just moved back to the US from Tokyo, and he had spent more than a handful of years in other Asian countries—places I'd lived and spent a lot of time. He was perfect on paper, but I was on alert because I felt like pieces were missing, like he wasn't telling me a lot of his stories and adventures.

One day I asked him outright how he managed to stay single. He cautiously explained that he could adapt *there* better than she could *here* in the US. I called it; he left his love in Thailand. He said he couldn't bring her home and used a myriad of excuses like not the right optics, work challenges, not fitting into social circles. Wow! So now, he dated women who were more acceptable on the surface. And he chose that over standing up for his love. That's why I ended up feeling bad for him. Poor him. Poor me! Waste of time *and* bad, bad, bad kissing.

Dating Outside the Zone

Lord Contradiction isn't a bad guy. There's something attractive about dating people you don't think are your type. How do you know your type unless you experiment?

You might be saying to yourself that Terresa's Lord Contradiction, Mr. Tall, Brunette, and Catholic, should get credit for being open to dating someone who was *not at all* who he was looking for, right? No! Sure, he was clear when asked, but he hadn't done his own homework. You've got to do the heavy lifting of knowing what you want and then be intentional about who you date to get there, especially when your intention is to find someone to share your life with.

I've got to unpack this a little. In my Lord Contradiction's case, the brunette thing? Easy fix. The tall part? No. The Catholic part? That's about foundational values and beliefs that don't just change. Hmmm. He was an amazing person, but I wasn't what he was looking for. I'd like to think that after me, he started dating tall, brunette Catholics and is now happily married with the family he always wanted. Maybe I helped him define and get back to his desired zone.

But even at the time, we were not young. He was a few years older than me, and I was in my mid-thirties. It's not like we were young guns coming out of high school and trying to figure out who we were and what we wanted. At that point, we were two fully developed humans who should have known better. At some point, if you want more than just a date, it's got to be a little bit more intentional and thought through for yourself.

At a certain point, if you just want a date, then you need to make sure you're not dating somebody who wants a family tomorrow. And if you want a partner, then you don't need to be dating some guy who's just out for dating. And you don't know until you ask.

As you get older and have more experience, the homework becomes easier. The self-actualization and understanding of who you are and what you need or want in a partner become more focused.

 As a woman, it's important to figure out what fits you, uncover what you want. How would you know you appreciate the quiet, calm guy if you only date the life of the party? It's the same with Lord Contradiction. Openness can be a good thing. It exposes you to more options and helps you define and fine-tune your choices.

Maybe it's just a stereotype, but I think women are classically trained to try and fit or contort themselves into what they think their partner wants.

I love the phrase "classically trained" in this context. Because we are. We've been groomed our entire life to fit society's molds. Maybe not the Gen Z'ers so much, although I could argue that Snap and TikTok are creating a different type of image compulsion, but women have been historically trained through magazines and TV and our friends and the world around us to know how to catch a man, catch a partner, keep a partner, and never actually check in with what you want and how you want to move.

 I'm sure you know girls like this: the guy they're dating loves camping. All of a sudden, your Four Seasons-loving, highly manicured friend owns a tent.

And maybe that's good. Maybe that's a growth thing. But if it's forced and false, that's not sustainable.

At the end of the day, compromise is everybody agreeing that there are two perspectives, and they both figure out how to give a little, and in the middle somewhere is the compromise. One person giving into somebody else is not compromise. It's giving in. It comes down to knowing yourself and being confident in who you are. Your own life's homework.

Lessons from Lord Contradiction

The key takeaway with this Lord is that you need to be direct and self-possessed. Are you clear about the type of person you want to date, so you can have prequalified candidates in the pipeline? Over time and with experience and intention, you'll get a lot better at articulating what you're looking for. It will save you a ton of time and emotional energy. This Lord should remind you why you need to be vigilant!

And when you do go on dates with these lucky candidates, ask them with confidence, "What's on your list?" Don't be afraid of the answer or that you won't measure up. It's an honest question looking for that honest answer.

Men have a list? Yes, believe it or not, men do have a list. It might exist only in their mind instead of in a journal they keep in their nightstand, but they have one, so ask! Then you'll be able to tell if they're Lord Contradiction or Lord My Guy.

5

LORD FOMO

"I saw on Facebook that the same woman keeps commenting on your posts and is a little flirtatious. It looks like you guys ran a 5k together recently. Are you dating her?"

I brace myself and continue, "Since I'm flying down to see you next weekend, I thought I better get this on the table now."

"Yeah, we go out," he says. "She's cool people."

FO·MO

/ˈfōmō/

noun

INFORMAL

1. anxiety that an exciting or interesting event may currently be happening elsewhere, often aroused by posts seen on social media; fear of missing out.

When you hear people say, "He's a catch, but he won't settle down," or, "Yeah, he's not ready for a real relationship yet," they're probably talking about Lord FOMO. Lord FOMO will even verify this Fear of Missing Out (FOMO) mentality by saying, "I don't want a relationship right now. I just want to have fun." And what does Lord FOMO say about the woman or man he's been seen with around town? "It's nothing serious," or, "We're just good friends."

That's Lord FOMO. Keeping all options open. But he's clear about the intention. This Lord doesn't keep anyone guessing for long and likely has a reputation of open or casual dating. Lord FOMO is certainly not secretive.

We know this Lord is playing the field because he says so. Many women will date Lord FOMO and say, "Surely, once he gets to know me, he'll change his mind. I can win him over." Uh, don't count on it.

Lord FOMO is who he says he is. Don't try to attach—because there are no strings.

"Hey, got a second?" I say sheepishly into the phone.

"Sure, what's up?" he says.

"I saw on Facebook that the same woman keeps commenting on your posts and is a little flirtatious. It looks like you guys ran a 5k together recently. Are you dating her?"

I brace myself and continue, "Since I'm flying down to see you next weekend, I thought I better get this on the table now."

"Yeah, we go out," he says. "She's cool people. I like her, but we're not exclusive."

"So, is it safe to say that you invited me down for the weekend, so you could see if I'm also worth an investment of your time?" I ask.

"I wouldn't say it like that, but basically, yes. It felt like we clicked in DC, and we had fun. I want to see if we click in real life."

Long pause, long pause. It took me a minute to check back into the conversation. I mean, was this man actually *honest?* I was waiting for the long, drawn-out story about how "There is nothing to see here," that she was just this girl he grew up with, or she was his barber's first wife's second cousin twice removed, so they are basically cousins too.

When I finally snapped back to the present, I said, "Cool, I just want to know what I'm workin' with. I don't like games. I'll see ya in a week!"

Lord FOMO might not be a crowd favorite, but I like this Lord! Why? Easy.

1. I don't have to guess. If I ask how this Lord rolls, he's truthful without spinning a wild tale created just to appease me.
2. He won't waste his time gaslighting me because he doesn't want the drama that comes along with disgruntled love interests. No mixed signals.
3. He's the guy who respects my agency over my own dating life. With Lord FOMO, I have enough information to make an informed decision and map my moves.

My Lord FOMO had *zero* strings hanging from his body. And when I found myself entering a season of open relationships, I looked to him for the playbook. He taught me how to be direct, genuine, kind, and *honest.*

I've tried it with Lord FOMO. I dated this guy. At least once. Okay, more than once. I met a Lord FOMO through a work connection. I know he had me pegged as a dull, white, blonde chick. We ran into each other when I had my hair all kinked out and was in a funky cocktail dress, just coming back from an event. Guess the hair changed his mind, and he decided to chase. Super fun. Serial dater. Not interested in commitment. He was very clear about that.

I was also very clear about wanting a relationship. I was looking for a partner. We had fun for a minute. I think he dated me because he saw me as seriously independent. In his mind, my independence signaled that I was moving the same way as he was. Like I was Lady FOMO.

Here's how I was sure: one afternoon, we were driving, and I said something about looking for a certain thing in my future partner. I swear his jaw dropped!

"What do you mean?" he said. "You don't want to get serious with anyone."

"What are you talking about? Of course, I do. Don't you?" I answered.

Fun over. What was I doing seeking a relationship with a Lord FOMO?!

A few years ago, I started seeing a doctor who was new in town—and the talk of the town. Within three months of his arrival, a girlfriend tried to set us up, but I shut it down. Doctors can be prima donnas. (Sorry to all my doctor friends. I do love you.) I had *no* time for that.

Turns out, I would meet this sexy surgeon at another friend's birthday party about a month later, and we hit it off and exchanged info. This guy was Lord FOMO, and I loved it.

This is what it looks like when Lady FOMO (me) meets Lord FOMO (the sexy doctor). We met for drinks and talked briefly about our backgrounds. We laughed at how resistant I was to meet him, let alone date him. We gently laid out our dating styles—not in some scrolled-up contract but loosely—and we began to see each other casually for months. On and off, here and there with no mention of status, other women or men, or what was next. It was perfect!

He's since moved to a neighboring city, and we keep in touch. He's a guy I could call to talk about my next venture or have a sexy night together with little to say. After either kind of encounter, we just say, "until next time."

Wait, We Have Questions!

Is a Lord FOMO a Lord FOMO forever? Or is this just a lightning-in-a-bottle moment? In other words, this year, he might be somebody I shouldn't approach for a relationship, but next year, he might be, right?

I don't know the answer, but the Lord FOMO in my opening story might be Lord FOMO for life. This is who he is, and this is how he lives. I've known him for almost ten years, and he's lived his whole life that way.

But I also think that people change and go through seasons like I have. I'm the female version of this, but I haven't always been that way. I was married. I've dated exclusively before. But now, I date openly. But I suspect I won't always approach my dating life like this. I think it's seasonal for me.

The question isn't whether Lord FOMO will always be that way; the question is, when you meet him, are you able to rock it out? Is this your match in this moment? Can you do this? And if the answer is *yeah, this sounds fun, and I can do this*, great. But if the answer is *hell no, I'm looking for more*, then don't get involved with Lord FOMO because he'll break your heart. That's the key. Know yourself.

How does somebody decide they're a Lord FOMO? How do you become a Lord FOMO? Is this guy damaged goods? Has he been in a bad relationship? Does he have a string of bad relationships? Is he wired this way, or has he never seen a good relationship?

My Lord FOMO definitely had some insight into himself. As cliché as this is going to sound, he had a lot of daddy issues. He watched his father run around and not invest in him or his mom. So, he stays away from committed relationships. For him, that's a real thing.

So, Lord FOMO is like Lord Fear, fear of more than just missing out. Fear of commitment.

Definitely. He lives his best life, right? He's super clear. With my Lord FOMO, if he made a decision to marry, that would be a big deal. We're such good friends that I would hope to be at his wedding because I would be so happy for him.

Well, that speaks to the honesty of this archetype. They're very clear. They're honest. No secrets. It is what it is. But you also just said, or inferred, that Lord FOMO is rare. Do you really think so?

I very rarely meet them. Here's the thing: Most men who date openly want to believe they are comfortable being honest about their approach, but when it gets down to it, they aren't. They don't want to hurt a woman by telling her the truth. They don't want to be totally honest because they want to keep their options open. They could lose somebody who's on the hook, and so they often fall into the category of Lord Layaway (more about him in the next chapter).

Lord FOMO is afraid of commitment, and he fears putting his whole self into something. He's afraid to take a chance because he might lose. Or he's afraid that he might not be great at it.

Do you think that somebody could actually be wired as a Lord FOMO?

I have a hard time buying it. I think you're right that it's all about timing. I don't believe Lord FOMO is an end state or even an innate, natural thing. I don't think we're wired that way as humans.

So, people like me place themselves in this category for a certain amount of time for whatever reasons. Maybe you're busy. Maybe a family member is sick. Maybe you've just moved cross country, and you don't want to go all-in on a relationship because you just got there.

 Right. You'll avoid a lot of hardship and heartache by saying, "Hey, right now is not the time." And then, take time to make sure you're where you want to be mentally, emotionally, physically, etc. When you're ready, you'll know what's out there.

Like after a divorce. When you get divorced, your next person is automatically your rebound person. That probably won't be your forever person. Accept that. Just be a Lord or Lady FOMO. You've just been through a lot of trauma. Even in the easiest of divorces, it's still an event. So, you probably need to date openly and be intentional about it.

 You can actually enjoy this approach; you might like the idea of dating.

Which brings us to another challenge: Women don't know how to date. My girlfriends struggle with dating and the mixed messages that can accompany it. Many women think they have to be with one person at a time. Every person they grab hibachi with is obviously "the one." After the first date, many women feel like there's some weird exclusivity or that they're going to be like, "Look, if you're not going to only date me, then I don't want to see you." They get scared. That's why Lord FOMO is rare.

To be Lord FOMO, it takes practice and requires skilled communication, directness, and some levity. You have to be able to approach this lightly so that other people don't take it personally. That's how I do it. I move with a lot of humor, and people take it or leave it. Mostly, they'll take it. Until they don't.

Lessons from Lord FOMO

Listen, Lord FOMO is playing the field and playing it honestly, so if you want a relationship, you probably don't want to deposit any long-term capital into this Lord.

Keep your eyes and ears open and accept what Lord FOMO says as the truth. The last thing you should do with Lord FOMO is interpret answers. Don't be tempted to think, *I'll win this Lord over,* 'cause honey, timing is everything! And if this Lord is not in it to win it and tells you that, believe it. And *please* don't get Lord FOMO's name tattooed on your lower back.

6

LORD LAYAWAY

"My name's not Candie."

"Whaaaaat? I didn't say Candie!"

"Are you kidding me? We're sitting a foot away from each other; you just called me Candie."

"I didn't say Candie. I said Jes," he protests. "You just hear what you want to hear."

lay·a·way

/ˈlāəˌuh wā/

noun

1. a system of paying a deposit to secure an item for later
   purchase. "She picked up a coat she had **on layaway.**"

nevitably, when you meet Lord Layaway, you think he's super charming, fun, and interesting. But Lord Layaway is code for *Lord Stay Away!* This Lord is your textbook *player*. Lord Layaway is driven by the chase but nothing else. This Lord's strengths are words, charm, promises (often broken), and, ultimately, the clever ability to keep you hooked. Lord Layaway will be all about you—in the beginning. Seriously, you might think you are the *only* one for this Lord. And then comes the manipulation and the deceit—and the gaslighting. Eventually, you find out that this Lord has other people on the hook, too, but by then, you've entered the game to win.

Lord Layaway loves the game. He loves juggling dates. Loves the drama created around the juggling; Lord Layaway feeds off of it. Know this: This Lord leaves a wake. Lord Layaway hurts people.

Girl, you better RUN!

"My name's not Candie."

"Whaaaaat? I didn't say Candie!"

"Are you kidding me? We're sitting a foot away from each other; you just called me Candie."

"PHUMPF . . ." (Phumpf is that one second audible sound made right before a landslide of excuses. It includes the inner thoughts of *Shit, I got caught. Now what am I going to say?*)

"I didn't say Candie. I said Jes," he protests. "You just hear what you want to hear."

"Oh, Hell-naw (expletive)! Have you lost your damn mind? The last thing you're going to do is make me think I'm crazy! You literally just sat here and called me another woman's name! You said it. I heard it. And you're not going to turn this on me.

"I hear what I want to hear, huh? Well, hear this: We're *done!*"

Candie, right? Sadly, this is a true story. What's also true is that I continued seeing this guy for several years after. One explosive encounter after another, fueled by similar lies and encouraged by his gaslighting and my need to be chosen, my need to win.

So, how does layaway work? Most of you probably think of layaway as that very antiquated buying habit, and you are right. For our readers born after 1990, layaway was a popular marketing and buying strategy for most retail outlets—and it's making a comeback. Long before online shopping made it easy to pull up multiple browser tabs and take advantage of free delivery, we put our dreamy, high-priced purchases on layaway. We visited them, petted them, tried them on again . . . at the store until we could, or decided to, make the final purchase.

Example: Imagine you're out shopping for a fifty-inch plasma TV, and you find a great option at the big box store down the road. What do you do? Naturally, you check out the features, the price, the design, etc. You imagine how it will look in your bonus room, and you finally decide to take it off the shelf. But you *don't buy it*, at least not now.

Yep, you heard me. When you shop on layaway, you physically take the product you want off the shelf, and it goes behind the counter with your name on it. You stop in once a week or once a month and make regular payments on it with the goal to pay it off by the terms of the layaway agreement. Meanwhile, since you haven't actually purchased the TV, you're compelled to keep looking to see if there are other deals out there that call your name. You can visit it. You can review it. You just don't take it home yet.

This practice assumes that you're willing to risk a small deposit to have the flexibility of buying a big-ticket item over time. Retailers bet that you'll pay full price, eventually, under flexible terms. Otherwise, you'll forfeit the deposit and any other payments made. This arrangement appeals to customers who are either fickle or don't have the upfront capital to invest. In the end, if you don't complete the purchase, the retailer keeps the deposit and the now older, possibly less relevant item. It's a savvy marketing strategy if everyone knows the risks.

In the same way that you might place that TV on layaway, this Lord places you—and his other ladies, unbeknownst to you—on layaway. The process starts off innocently enough and mirrors other relationship beginnings. But soon, the norms start to change, and Lord Layaway breaks out the playbook. It begins by putting $5 down to take you off the market and hold you "in the back."

You might ask, "How does this $5 investment show up in a relationship?" He'll call or text sweet or naughty messages during the day and insist on seeing you, but most of this will be on his terms and with very few specifics. His $5 deposit is just enough to signal that you're wanted but without real assurances of what's happening behind the scenes.

This form of hot and cool messaging gives our Lord the time to keep looking. He's got you off the shelf and on hold. You're steadily trying to figure him out, dreaming about the possibilities, and checking in with girlfriends to interpret his cryptic text messages. Meanwhile, he's still out shopping, looking for a different, maybe better, deal in another store. He's back to his routine, reading the reviews and trying out a different model, and guess what? If he likes what he sees, he'll put her (Candie) on layaway too, and so on and so forth. This Lord *loves* options and the chase that ensues, but his honesty meter is broken.

Inevitably, the women he's placed on the shelf get fed up with his split attention and his lies, and they want more. Here's where you'd imagine that it all falls apart and everyone wises up. But not so fast. This is the point where the stakes get raised. As soon as the alarms go off that she's getting played, the woman confronts the tension between getting off the crazy train and wanting to win. Many of us choose the latter. Take me, for instance. I competed against Candie—and others—for years.

So, if the woman stays in the game to win, what's in it for our Lord? To be sure, Lord Layaway enjoys the higher stakes too. This new level makes the thrill of the chase more intense. He fuels this dysfunctional relationship with expert gaslighting and manipulation. He'll take his lies and double talk to the absolute edge, and just when you're about to walk, he'll pull back to make you second-guess if you were just imagining his bad behavior. Confusion reigns! Lord Layaway keeps his conquests in a constant state of confusion. They never really know what's going on.

Lord Layaway is different from Lord FOMO because Lord FOMO is direct and clear. Lord Layaway is anything but. Dating Lord Layaway is never a good idea. It's way more trouble than it's worth, which is why we suggest you "Run, Forrest, run" if you're dating this Lord.

 I definitely dated this guy. He was accomplished, funny, good-looking, charming, coy, and distant, which I interpreted as mysterious and interesting at the time. He totally made me feel like I was "the one," the only one, when I was with him, or when *he* wanted attention. Then I wasn't. At all.

He was totally about himself, even when he was trying to make me think it was about me. I didn't date this guy for that long, but it was still too long. I could never figure out where I stood with him. It was too hard. It felt like a competition. I kept thinking, *Wow, I'm in it to win it.* And for a little while, I wanted to win without even being sure of the prize. But then I got tired of the runaround. Lack of direct answers, lack of ability to plan. Total inability to trust him, even with basic logistics.

In moments of self-reflection, I could see the game he was playing with all the deception. It had to be exhausting to juggle so many people. It's crazy, but at the same time, I have to admit, I was trying to win. I've also decided that I didn't like this guy as a person. Who he was authentically was just *off*. He was always going and doing, but you could never get a straight answer about who he was with or where he went.

If I invited him to something, it was always some form of "maybe" or some drama he'd have to go through to "make it work." This Lord Layaway also fits Lord Self-Absorbed (you'll meet him in another chapter), but what drives him is his "Player with a capital P" self. Manipulation and deceit are his lifeblood.

I actually knew he was a player, but I didn't acknowledge the manipulation and deceit in our relationship. When we were together, it was glorious. I felt on top of the world. But that wasn't most of the time. So, while not soon enough, I walked away. Very confused.

 The last Lord Layaway I dated confused me too—so much so that I haven't fully processed our time together. I entered our relationship honestly and with two requests:

1. I didn't want to be in a relationship where I was held to a lot of expectations. I needed my schedule to remain unencumbered and fluid. It wasn't the season for me to be on the phone every day for hours or to fly to see him every other weekend (or once a month, for that matter.) We lived in different states, so our geography was a natural barrier.

2. I needed him to know that I would likely date other people or at least would exercise the option to do so, and he would have the same opportunity. In other words, I wanted our relationship to be open (Lady FOMO).

Now, you would think this would be a guy's *dream* scenario. He's got a girl who doesn't need all the fuss and is comfortable with him dating other women as long as she can date other men. Touchdown! Win-win! A dream come true—but apparently not.

Despite the fact that I was clear about what I wanted in the relationship, Lord Layaway reared his ugly head. With all this freedom, he still managed to lie, cheat, and manipulate his way through our relationship. I don't think he believed that I would actually be okay with him dating someone else. So, to make sure I didn't go anywhere, he acted like I was his girlfriend while lying about the other women he dated, the trips he took, and even the existence of other women at all. It was unnecessary. I think the freedom to date openly was a new experience, and he didn't trust the process. At the end of the day, he didn't trust me. And I couldn't trust him.

It's interesting that on more than one occasion, I've experienced the shock that accompanies my ability to navigate open relationships. I've been called "the man" in the relationship, which, as you can imagine, is childish and clearly sexist. Why do men assume that they can handle dating at arm's length, but women can't? Why do they assume that women are emotionally fragile? Trust me, I *can* handle it. If anything, the men I date are the ones who fall apart in the end.

 Wow, Jes. That brings up a whole other conversation—our next book? *Why Men Can't Handle Equitable Behavior in Women?* Certainly, that attitude is not exclusive to Lord Layaway. And not, I think, the primary driver for Lord Layaway. I don't think this Lord is worried about his women handling anything. It's more about him. Lord Layaway is not likable. Deceit and manipulation are his prime characteristics—two very unlikable qualities. And, in thinking about my story, it's a little hard to admit that I didn't like who he was at his core.

 Why is that hard to admit?

 Because he was charming, and he was fun, and he was desirable, and there was a chase involved. And I wanted to 'win'. I chased. I chased this guy I didn't even like. Yuck. If you're with a Lord Layaway, you're always chasing somehow. You're always trying to get purchased in full. So, there's that competition factor. I had to admit I was chasing a guy I didn't even like. It's amazing how I fooled myself into thinking that looking great together on paper and the charm and fun in the moment were enough without looking deeper. And then once I looked deeper, I thought, *What the hell am I doing with this person?*

That's exactly what I was going to say. For me, it feels like these guys are an indictment against *me*. I know they aren't, but it feels like an indictment against my own judgment.

That's why it's uncomfortable to say that Lords Layaway are nasty people.

And I spent a lot of time with these types of men. The truth is, there isn't one that I like either. At the bitter end, you honestly couldn't be with them if you wanted to because they intentionally hurt you and put their needs first.

It begs the question: what's happening within yourself at the time? This Lord requires you to be introspective. And that's scary too, to figure out why you keep gravitating to Lords Layaway. How many of these guys did you date?

Oh, more than a couple.

Okay, so it's not just me.

Oh. No. They are seriously charming. Coveted. The other thing that makes this uncomfortable is that I, like you, am a people person. It's my nature to give people the benefit of the doubt. So, it's hard for me to think there are a ton of these guys out there. I don't want to believe it. But it's true; there are a ton of Lords Layaway. The deceit. The manipulation. The lies. The games. All alive and well and thriving. And using the words *deceit* and *manipulation* feels harsh when you're just saying, "Oh, he plays games." But the truth is that the games *are* deceitful and manipulative.

Cheaters are Lords Layaway, even if they've "bought you" (e.g., you're married or "exclusive"). You might have a ring on your finger, but you're still on layaway with this guy.

 Yes, because he's putting money down on other women, so you're not the full picture for this guy.

 Do you think this Lord is born or built this way? Or could this simply be behavior in a moment in time?

 In my experience, every Lord Layaway I've known is still that way. I know you don't stay in contact with your past people. You cut those cords and moved on. But I still have a line to all but one of them. I check in to say, "Merry Christmas. We're all fine," etc. So, I see it.

In a few cases, they're dating people I know. And I haven't seen redemption. I would love to see a redemption story, but I haven't.

 You say redemption, but because of who they are as people, they clearly don't think they need redemption. They don't need it. This is their way of being. This is their way of operating.

 Here's where I think redemption comes in. I believe that people have that better side, that better angel. Lords Layaway leave a wake. They hurt people. And when you do that enough, and you've created enough chaos around you and in other people's lives, those who have that better angel see they're responsible for it. But it takes ruining lives, being very destructive, toxic, all that stuff. It's almost like they have to cause enough pain and chaos to see the damage they've caused to want redemption.

 I want to make sure that when we're talking about married or dating and cheating or lying that we're clear about the differences between an *archetype* and a *behavior*. Everyone can make a mistake, and it's not necessarily part of who they are or their M.O. It could simply be a bad behavior at that moment, like if you're dating somebody and you make a mistake and end up cheating on them somehow. That doesn't necessarily mean you're Lord Layaway.

Yes, I agree. If cheating was the qualifying action to make you Lord Layaway, then I could be considered

Lady Layaway because I've cheated. But that's not how I'm driven; deceiving and manipulating men to get what I need out of a relationship is not my motivator. Yes, when I cheated, it was a poor decision, but it was circumstantial for sure. But for the Lord Layaway archetype, the control drives them. That's what gets them off.

So, why are you still in touch with your Lords Layaway—or all your ex-boyfriends for that matter?

It's probably how I'm wired. I'm not in touch with any of them with a secret desire to reconnect. Hardly! But there's something about every man I've dated that I liked initially—their intelligence, their drive, their ambition. I still admire those parts of who they are.

In some cases (not all), I absolutely abhor how they handled our relationship. And they all know. They all recognize that. But I still care about them even though the doors are closed.

By the way, you absolutely need to close doors. That's important to hear. You know the guy who was seeing both Candie and me at the same time? It took me nine years to fully close that door. That's hard to admit, but I think there are many women who can relate to that. If you get clear on your value, your worth, it doesn't have to take that long.

Lessons from Lord Layaway:

- You don't know you're on layaway because you think you're the big purchase. And here's the crazy part; you keep competing to be that prize.
- When you realize you're on layaway with all the other women, you can't tell for sure if large or small deposits are being made on your behalf, and therefore, you're inclined to wait it out to see if you're the lucky winner.
- If you're dating Lord Layaway, you're probably giving him exactly what he wants while you spiral into a ball of confusion, self-doubt, and insecurity. You think you're playing the same game, but you're playing by different rules. Lord Layaway is not a Lord to be won.
- While relationships with Lord Layaway aren't healthy, they don't have to be self-destructive if caught early.
- Walk away. Actually, *run!*

Blooper: Poof! He's Gone

We met at this amazing bar in San Francisco, super posh. It had a dark, old library feel. He was already there with a drink in hand when I arrived. I sat down and ordered my beer from a waiter. I was so excited because they had a Belgian beer that I hadn't seen on a menu outside of Belgium.

He asked if I was up for a quiz.

"Sure," I said, and so it began.

"Picture a cube on a big screen," he said. "What size is the cube? Now, picture a ladder. Where does the ladder reach the cube? Now, a horse. Is it leashed or not?"

Yes. He asked if the horse was on a leash. True story.

"Now, picture rain. When you think of rain, what does your rain look like? Next, picture flowers. What kind of flowers?" And so on.

This whole time, I thought we were having a fun, albeit weird, conversation. We were sitting in these loungey-type swivel chairs, mostly facing each other. Then the guy starts sweating. One of his arms goes up and wraps around his neck, so his chin is in the crook of his elbow. The sweat was streaming down his face. Gradually, his elbow moved up, so it was covering his mouth. Buckets of sweat. Sweat and more sweat. Raining sweat. He started sinking into his chair.

In less than fifteen minutes, the waiter came by to ask if we needed anything. I turned slightly to respond—and ask for my check. I turn back to the guy, and he was gone. Just gone. Poof!

Blooper: LinkedIn

He messaged me on LinkedIn and invited me on a date. His message was simple, clear, and compelling. We met for drinks at 21c in Durham, where he became forward, assumptive, and gross, and trust me, I'm not a prude.

The next day, I had dinner with my best friend and told her about the date and how we met. When I used his first name, she said, "Wait. Ben XXXX?"

I was like, "Uh yeah," followed by, "Did you sleep with him?"

Now, this is a funny, girlfriend-code question where you're half kidding, and it's normally followed by, "Girl, no!" But my girlfriend threw her head back in the chair and buried her face in her hands.

"Remember the guy I told you about last year that I met at a red light?" she said.

Yep, she'd actually met Ben when he came up next to her at a red light. They pulled over, exchanged numbers, and kicked it for a short time. When she learned that he was married, it soured the deal.

I said, "Wait, married! Is he still married?"

"Yep, as far as I know."

And on that note, we took a picture together and sent it to him. C'est la vie, Ben!

Blooper: Charles—er, maybe Chuck

Charles
~~Stanford Physicist~~ ⚠ Self-described

🎓 **Education**
~~Stanford~~ ⚠ Lives near Stanford

ℹ️ **Info**
~~Active spontaneous guy with a good~~ ⚠ Unemployed
~~work/play balance~~
~~Divorced~~ ⚠ 3x
~~Educated~~ ⚠ ...Sure?

BLOCK & REPORT

I walk into Il Fornaio, San Francisco, to meet Charles, the Stanford Physicist. We had set up a date just for drinks. Charles is highly educated, has a great work/life balance, and enjoys life spontaneously. He believes in marriage and relationships. And he prides himself on being real with people.

My determination?

- Stanford Physicist = He maybe lives in the general area of Stanford and knows how to spell physics. (Okay, I'm cruel! Whatever.)
- Good work/play balance = He has three part-time jobs.
- Active/spontaneous = He has no full-time job.
- Believes in marriage = He was divorced multiple times; it could even be a habit.
- Contractor in his spare time = He's a handyman for his part-time employers.
- Authentic = He has no filter and is rough around the edges. All of them.

Charles = Chuck.
But . . . likely a good guy.

Blooper: Tom Petty

"There's a Tom Petty concert this weekend. Do you want to go?" John asked.

"Um, okay. What does he sing again? I mean, I know the name Tom Petty, but I don't really know his music. Remind me—what's one of his hits?"

John laughed. "Free Fallin'. Everyone knows that one!"

I met John at the pool in our apartment complex that summer. My son and I moved there after my husband and I separated, and we became fast friends. He was fun and kind and white. Now, I don't discriminate, so dating a white man, yellow man, purple man is not off the table. But, it seems, I'm 99 percent attracted to Black men. So, when John asked me to this concert, I was like, "Yeah, let's roll, friend!"

So, we did. We rolled up to the dusty, overcrowded parking lot and found our way onto the lawn. We plopped down on our blanket, and it dawned on me that his friends were all coupled up. By the second song of the opening act, yikes, I was on an accidental date, and I made up the second half of our couple.

Damn, how'd I miss that? Bottomline, I felt trapped in a *Lifetime* movie and getting a contact high to boot. This American Girl was ready to go home.

Blooper: Can You Pick Me Up?

"Hey, can't wait to see you. Can you swing by and pick me up?"

That gem of a text came about thirty minutes before I was headed to meet this fly, charming, and aspiring hip-hop artist for drinks. *You mean, you've been texting me and planning our date for the last two days and failed to mention that you don't have a car?*

And instead of figuring it out, you ask me—thirty minutes before the date—to "swing by" and pick you up?

My answer to that bullshit text was something like, "No."

This wasn't just about the lack of transportation, though not ideal. I was more irritated by the timing—the disregard for my time. While I'm unconventional in many regards, I'm traditional when it comes to transportation, manners, and chivalry. Sure, he was a starving artist, but he seemed more focused on his brand than on being a responsible, grown-ass man.

Get your life together, sir!

Period. Full stop.

Blooper: Dive vs. Jump

I was on a tropical vacation with friends for a big event, and my new-ish, super-comfortable-in-the-water boyfriend and I were on a big party boat.

"Hey, let's go to the top (third level) and dive off," my hulking Aussie says.

"Great. I'm in."

I was chatting to everyone we passed as we were going up top, not paying much attention. Then I put down my drink and dove in after him. I came out of the water, and he was furious!

"How could you make me look so bad!?"

"What?"

Apparently, he jumped. I didn't even know.

I dove.

Big red flag. You know those girlfriends who disappear on tropical islands, and the boyfriend has no idea what could have happened? (It must have been a boating or swimming accident. Yeah right.) Well, I'll say it again.

Big red flag!

Blooper: I Love You ... Right Now

Full disclosure, this is not my story, but it's too good not to tell. I've had the great fortune to have fun, amazing neighbors in my life. One of them was always good for a hysterical dating story. Nearly every week.

So, my neighbor comes up to my flat, walks in, goes down the hall to the refrigerator, grabs a beer, and says, "Oh god, I think I messed up."

"Tell me more," I say.

"Well, last night, we (she and Craigslist Casual Encounters Guy) were really hot and heavy. Serious good sex. As we were into it and kissing, he says, 'I love you'!"

"Oh my god! You haven't known him long (at all)! You're in the middle of sex—what did you do?" I ask.

"I didn't want to mess up the mood. And I didn't want to lie. So, I said 'I love you, right now.'"

Blooper: Attorney Match

I met this gem on Match.com. His profile photo was very attractive, albeit clearly outdated. No bother, I thought. He might age like Denzel, which worked for me. According to his profile, he was an attorney and former U of Miami college football player. His profile went on to say that he'd recently moved back to North Carolina from Indiana to take care of his mom and practice law in Greensboro. No red flags, right?

We met at a Starbucks off Route 85. I walked in and saw a six-foot-three-inch, 399-pound Black man crammed in a corner table reading a hardbound book that was easily four inches thick. Other than college, I had never seen anyone reading a book of such size in public. As we began our date, he explained that this book featured the classics—*Moby Dick, Great Gatsby, Catcher in the Rye,* and others. I blanked out after discussing his literary preferences for fifteen minutes.

He was awkward and uncomfortable, clearly trying too hard. He shared that he was living with his mom while he started up his practice in North Carolina. While I processed that, I couldn't help but notice that he had not evolved into Denzel. In fact, time had not been kind to him at all. This online bait-and-switch pissed me off. Just be honest! Lying about what you look like online wins the ladies over every time, said no one ever! I mean, your secret's out the exact moment we lay eyes on you. Ugh.

When I got home, the weirdness of the date and my annoyance turned to anger, and I became more curious about what was going on with this guy. So, I did what any self-respecting online dater would do—I Googled him.

Turns out he was disbarred in Indiana and was living with his mom for his benefit, not hers. We parted with such sweet sorrow—not!

Blooper: What NOT to Do on a Date with a Rock Star—or Anyone Else

A friend of a friend set me up with a Rock Star. Yep, a bonafide Rock Star. He'd made it in music. It took a while to connect, but when he finally reached me for a quick, first meetup, I was very happy to jump right in. After all, I'd been day-drinking, so why not? "Let's meet tonight!" What could possibly go wrong? Oh boy.

In my super confident, very happy drunkenness, we covered politics, religion, and every other taboo subject over a couple of me-being-overly-familiar hours.

The next day I thought, *That was fun! What a great, comfortable guy.*

I never heard from him again.

Blooper: How Can I Get His Number . . . For My Friend

I was set up with this guy by my dating agent. The deal is that, after you meet, you and your date have to decide whether to exchange contact information. The dating agent doesn't give it to you. They just tell you where and when to meet your date.

So, I was with this guy. Just a quick meetup for drinks. Turns out, he's intelligent, accomplished, and works in psychiatry. I learned that he liked camping, weekend trips, classical music, blue grass, meditation, and world travel. We had a fun conversation around psychoanalysis and dating—and his work.

I was seriously distracted while he was talking because . . .

He was super interesting . . .

Super attractive . . .

Seemed fun . . .

All the things . . .

The whole time, I'm thinking, *Wow, this guy would be perfect . . .*

. . . for my friend.

I suck as a date. I didn't even get his info to pass along.

Blooper: Your Friends Sound Great

I met this guy for a drink at a cool, hip café. According to him, he was active, kindhearted, loyal, compassionate, passionate, and interesting.

He had some great stories and adventures to tell. He also made sure I knew he had a huge friend network, was a baseball player, and loved the game.

Well, a leopard always shows his spots. In a short amount of time, I learned that he hadn't played baseball since high school. He did go to the gym—sometimes. All his stories were *other people's stories*. He was the bystander. The observer.

In a nutshell: Fun guy that does a ton of stuff = Guy willing to watch other people do a lot of their fun stuff. I wanted to date his friends!

Blooper: Pride for $1,000

A few years back, I got a text from a girlfriend who was on a business trip in Atlanta. She'd met the perfect guy for me and wanted to make an introduction. I was intrigued and said, "Why not?"

She described him as being over six feet tall (6'6" to be exact), funny, personable, very handsome, former military, successful, and studying for his PhD. The fact that he was also "out of market" was enough to give this matchmaking effort a thumbs up.

She patched us together over text, and we were off and running. We talked and texted regularly, and within six weeks, I made my way to Atlanta, so we could formally meet.

Day One. We met for dinner and drinks downtown and talked for two hours. He was *everything* he appeared to be on social media. He was gorgeous and had a body like no other; he seriously looked like a G.I. Joe action figure. And he was kind.

The only pause I took that night was from the crumbs he threw out about being fairly conservative and a little judgmental. Once in a while, he'd bring discipline and hard work into the conversation and say he had little patience for people who were down on their luck.

"They should just apply themselves and make their way in the world, save money, and prosper."

Yes, in a perfect world, that made sense, and if that was all it took, we wouldn't have a socioeconomic divide. Was he unaware of systemic oppression? I digress. Overall, day one was not bad.

Day Two. He picked me up and took me to his beautiful new home in the suburbs. He cooked, and it was perfect. After dinner, he suggested we watch TV together. I was in for a nice relaxing evening to cuddle, drink wine, and watch a movie or a series.

Uh, no. He wanted to challenge me to a game of Jeopardy, his favorite show. Now, I liked Alex Trebek (God rest his soul) as much as the next girl, but this was not Netflix and Chill. This was Game On and Compete! Atlanta Boo was so serious and so competitive that near the end, I got tired of him shouting the answers over me and started checking my IG account. True to form, he made me play until the final round just to satisfy his ego.

He was proud of his mind, his accomplishments, and his life. I wouldn't have cared about that night if I hadn't gotten a sneaky suspicion that the apex of his joy and happiness was his pride. When he was winning and in control, he was content.

We never saw each other again. We talked only when he had time. He was very clear he'd be off the radar to write and defend his dissertation, which was his priority. I obliged willingly. I was in Atlanta a lot over the next few months and would let him know I was coming down. Each time, he'd respond with, "Call when you get here." But I never did, and he could never bring himself to ask why not.

I'll take "Ego Trip" for $1,000.

7

LORD SELF-ABSORBED

 I landed at the evening mixer and moved from table to table to introduce myself. I walked up to a certain table and said, "Hi."

The guy sitting immediately to my right wrapped his hand around my bare calf.

I turned and looked him in the eye, like "What the hell are you doing?"

He kept his hand on my calf, and I let him.

self-ab·sorbed

/ˌself-əbˈzôrbd/

adjective

1. preoccupied with one's own feelings, interests, or situation.

This Lord is so in love with himself that there really isn't time for you—unless you're turning the glow back on him. This Lord is great. Just ask him! Oh, wait; you won't have to ask. He'll happily share. Lord Self-Absorbed is unapologetically confident in himself and in his accomplishments, maybe deservingly so. In turn, this Lord is going to expect you to be accomplished and confident too.

No matter what you bring to the table, the spotlight will eventually fall back on this Lord. No matter what. When you tell Lord Self-Absorbed something about your day, he'll immediately jump in with something about his day. This Lord is not a listener, except for the cues that signal him to interject himself.

We're not going to say that this Lord is narcissistic. That's Lord At-Your-Peril. This Lord is pretty harmless. Self-centered, but harmless. So, Lord Self-Absorbed borders on narcissism but doesn't cross the line.

 My experience with Lord Self-Absorbed: It was summer in Southern California, and I was representing my agency at a negotiating skills training conference. After a long day, I landed at the evening mixer and moved table to table to introduce myself and my agency over beer. I walked up to a certain table and said, "Hi."

The guy sitting immediately to my right wrapped his hand around my calf. I turned and looked him in the eye, like "Uh!" I think he was just as surprised as me that he'd done that. But he kept his hand on my calf, and I let him. This was the beginning of a summer of nearly perfect dates.

He was a total blast—as long as everything went his way. And looked the right way. To be fair, he knew he was self-absorbed. And I knew it. This Lord was a successful entrepreneur. Tall, dark, and handsome. He'd just sold his business to the parent company of the agency I worked for. He was total confidence. Total appeal. Divorced. Feeling his full self. We dated long distance, which suited us both. He was into me because of my positions and the lifestyle I was living. He liked the look of it. But if any of that façade had changed, our worlds would no longer have fit together. That much was clear. We might have even said that out loud to each other.

We took turns planning the perfect dates for each other over a long summer. Suite in a high-rise in Vegas, box show seats, exclusive club access. Lots of little details. No care in the world. All the travel and logistics worked perfectly. Delays were not in our program. Upgrades everywhere just showed up. Dressed to kill. Both of us. Champagne the perfect temp. Unplanned, lighting made us look and feel ten years younger. You know. The stuff you can write but maybe never believe can be real. Every moment scheduled with some hard-to-find ticket/hard-to-get access. We looked great together. All the things: perfection.

After several of those quick, perfect weekends away, he invited me to fly in to spend a weekend at his home. I thought, *Okay, so maybe we're getting to know each other now.* Wrong! (Did I mention we were so scheduled on our perfect dates that we didn't ever really have time to get to know each other?) He wanted me to see all the great things he was developing on his property. Eesh. We had fun, but we never got to know each other beyond the surface. Or rather, he didn't get to know me at all. There was no real sharing. He clearly didn't want that. But we did have a series of pretty perfect dates, and that's where it ended.

 I dated this Lord too; he was my Oakland Boo. As a serial entrepreneur, he found success early on—very early on. He'd sold his first company after college, just before the dot.com bubble burst, and he'd made a lot of money. This type of unique success can lead a person to believe he is unusually gifted, anointed, and/or operating at a higher frequency than those around him.

Of course, he would never admit this, but he wore a halo, and it made him difficult to date. Our conversations became predictable. The way he engaged was to bring his past glories and future business conquests into every discussion whenever possible, and I could tell when it was coming.

So, why would I date him? It seems like he'd be an easy read, right? Well, not at first. Let's be clear; he was a smart, ambitious, and self-sufficient man. He was handsome, tall, and a good dad. He drew me in. He was also kind and generous. He did the right things because men who win big pull out the "How to Win a Girl in 30 days" playbook and run those plays beautifully. But when it came down to the little things, like being vulnerable and thinking about me voluntarily, he fumbled.

How can I put this? While Oakland Boo didn't have a strong air of overt arrogance, he was covered in a haze of superficiality. It was always about his next venture, his deals, his strategy, and his approach.

And, like a guy in sales, he had one-liners, inspirational quotes, and mantras for days:

"You can't be what you can't see!"

"You are the average of the five people you spend the most time with."

"What you focus on is what you get."

. . . and we rarely went beyond the first few plays. Game over.

It seems silly to ask, "What drives them?" because it seems so obvious. It's their ego, right?

I think it's two things: their ego and their lived experience. My guy had tasted success early in life, which led him to become self-important. He obviously thought *he* was the reason for his success. I think he created a scenario where as long as he was the key to every relationship, everything would be successful.

That's got to be stressful! I mean, seriously, to have to carry the whole thing all the time?

Yes, that approach doesn't leave a lot of room for you to be in the equation, or maybe you'll always be second. He was the first variable, and you're the second—maybe a *distant* second variable. That's what success is for him.

Wow. What about the ego component? In my example, there was absolute ego and "I'm great" involved. And the facades—his and mine—were incredibly important to him.

Do you think they're born this way? Or is it a moment in time? You talked about life experience, so that leads me to think that you believe it's learned behavior.

I don't think it's a moment in time. And I don't think they were born this way. I think that once they've established this habit of self-absorption, that's who they are. In my case, I didn't want to change him, and I wasn't willing to put up with it.

You mentioned a playbook in your story, a "How to Win a Girl in 30 Days Playbook." That's awesome. So, does this playbook really exist? What is it?

Ha! I joke about this because my Lord Self-Absorbed was a damn good salesman in real life. He didn't come off as super selfish, and he did all the right things for a while. Looking back, it seemed like I was a part of a dating "sales pipeline" or "playbook." The "How to Win a Girl in 30 Days" is akin to the classic book *How to Win Friends and Influence People*. And when it appeared like I was along for the ride, his patterns shifted. Only then did it become obvious that it had always been about him and only him. By then, we were a month in, and that behavior change was confusing.

I picture the playbook including basic things like, "1) Touch base with your new prospect a few times a week via text or phone call. Don't wait for her to contact you. Show your interest and your ability to be consistent. 2) Use words like *we* and *us* when talking about the future, so she can imagine herself in your life. 3) When traveling to see her, always offer to get a hotel room; never ask to stay with her. Let her extend the invitation. Take caution and be prepared to actually book a room. She may be testing your sincerity. 4) If that happens, don't worry. Being a man of your word will win you big points, and you'll get that invitation next time."

After about thirty days of this gaslighting, the signs start to show up. That's when you start to say, "Oh, that was weird. I haven't seen that behavior before. Let me just ignore it." Or "Why is he talking about himself all the time now? I thought I had a part of this conversation. Maybe he's just excited about this venture." And you ignore it. All of a sudden, you've been dating him sixty days, and you're caught up in some kind of crazy game or superficial loop.

That leads me to the contrast with this guy and Lord At-Your-Peril, who we talk about in the next chapter. I don't see Lord Self-Absorbed as needing to be toxic. The world revolves around him, and he'd never think to abuse you because that would take his energy and attention away from himself.

You're more likely to see neglect from Lord Self-Absorbed than abuse. Neglect is where you feel unfulfilled in that relationship.

You and I have decided we can't be with this guy, but do you think Lord Self-Absorbed can maintain long-term relationships? Do you think there's a woman out there for this guy? I'm sure a lot of these guys are married, right?

 Oh, sure. They aren't out there spending Friday nights talking to themselves in the mirror. Lord Self-Absorbed could be fulfilling for someone. They find their person along the way. It can work.

 Yes. If you're both on board with what it is, I can see that it could work. It all comes back to knowing yourself and what you want.

We've begun to compare Lord Self-Absorbed with a narcissist (or Lord At-Your-Peril, who you'll meet in the next chapter), so let's talk about what they have in common and how they're different.

- **Focus on self.** Obviously, Lord Self-Absorbed is totally focused on self. A narcissist is also self-centered. People who've always been put on a pedestal or never disciplined can easily become narcissistic. If you're an only child, for example, and have been given a ton of attention, you can seem more self-centered than most because you never learned anything different. Not a huge differentiator by itself. You can't make a determination based only on self-focus.

- **Empathy.** Lord Self-Absorbed can feel remorse and change his behavior. For example, if you challenge this Lord for taking your last cookie without asking if you wanted it, he'll feel bad and do something to make up for it. A narcissist, however, will either dismiss you or get mad because you confronted him. With the narcissist, it becomes your fault that he took the cookie. Lord Self-Absorbed just wanted the cookie and didn't think about anybody else before taking it.
- **Ability to listen.** Lord Self-Absorbed may talk about himself too much, but he can also listen to others. Not so with narcissists. Not only do they not listen, but they also force you to listen to how special they are—and how special you're not.
- **Moral values.** Lord Self-Absorbed has clear moral values and mostly follows them. Narcissists think that rules don't apply to them.

Lessons Learned from Lord Self-Absorbed

- Lord Self-Absorbed can be tiresome and opinionated. It can be exhausting to spend all your time and energy appreciating how wonderful this Lord and his ideas are. Those who choose to be around Lord Self-Absorbed accept this Lord for who he is and have found their own ways to constructively continue their relationship, be it friendships or love interests.
- This Lord is not a giver or someone who can truly share. The world is about Lord Self-Absorbed. This Lord sees only one perspective, and that colors everything.

- Lord Self-Absorbed doesn't have to be toxic. But he can be a self-esteem buster because, most of the time, you won't feel like you are seen. It's not because this Lord is putting you down or taking away from you. It's just that it's never about you. And if you need that, you better look elsewhere.

- Cultivating a deep or quality relationship or friendship is hard work. If you're looking for a deep, personal partner, this is not your Lord.

8

LORD AT-YOUR-PERIL

He had a big birthday coming up, so I planned a surprise party.

Twenty-plus people flew in from all over the world for him. He and I walked up the Charles River to a dock where all his friends were on a party boat. They jumped up and yelled, "Surprise!" Success, you might say.

He looked at me with a big smile and quietly said, "You cunt!" and walked up the gangplank to greet his guests.

per·il

/ˈperəl/

noun

1. serious and immediate danger.

Lord At-Your-Peril is a predator. This Lord is abusive and can heap it on in a variety of ways: verbal, mental, emotional, or physical. But abuse is tricky. It rarely starts out feeling like abuse. It couldn't because you wouldn't stand for it. It's like the story about putting a frog in a pot of water. If the water's boiling, the frog jumps out. But if the water is cool and you gradually raise the temperature, the frog adjusts—and eventually cooks.

Abuse starts out as a negative word, a demeaning gesture. Maybe Lord At-Your-Peril is overprotective or dismisses you and your ideas. Or blames you for something you didn't do or cause. But, no big deal, right? It's something you can brush off and say this Lord was having a bad moment. Sometimes, it is *not* a big deal. Sometimes, it becomes a big deal. Sometimes, it morphs into abuse.

Avoid this Lord. If you already know Lord At-Your-Peril, then run! Get back to your people. Truly. The relationship won't get better. It can't because it's not about you. You didn't do anything wrong, and you can't fix it or this Lord. Over time, Lord At-Your-Peril will destroy tiny little bits of you until you don't recognize yourself. And the effects can be very long-lasting.

The worst cases of abuse end in death. They all end up with varying degrees of personal destruction and a deep need for healing.

The Boyfriend

I've often wondered, *How does a strong-willed, successful, opinionated woman become the subject of abuse?* Go back to the frog. The heat turns up slowly, and before you know it, you're cooked. I was involved with not one, but two Lords At-Your-Peril! I'm ashamed to admit this. I'm embarrassed. How stupid could I be? Not once, but twice! Very stupid. I feel it all. Even so, I want to tell you, so you can avoid this type of person.

A woman I was getting to know, someone I really liked and would have loved to develop a friendship with, asked me something about my then-boyfriend. She said to me, "What the hell? How do you take that?"

I brushed her off and said, "Ah, well, sometimes, your past prepares you to have better tolerance for things in the future."

I was talking about the sociopath I was living with. This is not an official diagnosis. It's my keen observation. But I don't use the word lightly. Yes, sociopath.

I was living outside the US when we got together. We'd been introduced by mutual friends and jumped into things pretty quickly. He was awkward but interesting. Intelligent. Successful. High functioning. I admired his curiosity. If he had a question about something, he'd research the answer, and this was before you could ask Siri or Alexa.

He was also insecure under all of that. He loved to make people (me) feel really, really small. He practiced it. Our maid was afraid of him. My dog was afraid of him. Eventually, I was afraid for us all.

He gave orders. He was a hulk of a guy. He used his physical presence. He used his powerful voice and his intellect and legal training to accuse and demean. Out with friends, he'd intentionally start fights with people. Some slight he felt. He'd make sure it involved me, so somehow, it was because of me that he'd be fighting with his mates. He got off on it. He could be mean. If you pissed him off and he wanted to be subtle, maybe your chair would weirdly slip out from under you, so you'd end up on the ground, sometimes taking other things and people with you. Then the story somehow became that you were an uncontrollable drunk, sliding out of your chair.

If you read the "Dive vs. Jump" story earlier in this book, this was him. When I came up out of the water, saw his fury, and saw him coming at me, I knew I had to seek people immediately. He was the one comfortable in the water. I was the one who was going to have an "accident". This was not a joke.

If you didn't do what he wanted, whether you knew what that was or not, he would corner you and physically and verbally threaten you. One time, I got between him and my dog as he was going for the dog's throat. I escaped with my pup down the back stairs while the housekeeper hid in her room and called a friend she knew at a veterinary office. They found an anonymous refuge for my dog for about a week (more than once) while things calmed down. We lived in an apartment on a high floor, and the whole front wall of glass opened up onto the balcony. Unfortunately, I know what the view is like looking down. I have no idea why our upstairs and downstairs neighbors didn't call the cops.

I didn't lose myself with him. I did, however, get way too caught up in trying to appease him, sometimes at the expense of others— always at the expense of myself. I didn't feel like I was a very good person at this time in my life. And I felt stuck. When I heard myself make excuses to that would-be friend, I started to wake up and examine my life. So, I left him, very quietly and quickly. I wrapped up my job and headed back to the States.

I got a call from him months later. When I returned to the US, I hadn't tried to hide from him, but I also wasn't advertising where I was living. When he tracked me down, it was an unpleasant surprise. We were half a world away from each other at the time, but I immediately called the local police to talk to them about my safety. It was a comforting conversation. And surprise—two officers showed up on my doorstep within twenty minutes. They thought it was serious enough to make a test run to my house, just so they'd know where I lived. They wanted me to know that they could get there in single-digit minutes if needed.

Silver lining? They were two super-cute men in uniform. (Gotta find the upside!)

Was I embarrassed? Yes. Was it sobering? Yes. Did I feel stupid? Yes. All those things and more ran through my head then and run through my head even now. Did I overreact by calling the police about something that I thought could happen to me by a man who was on the other side of the world? No. I don't think so. And given how seriously they took me, I don't think they thought I was overreacting either. That's how serious domestic violence is.

The Ex-Husband

Six years earlier, I walked away from my first marriage and my first encounter with Lord At-Your-Peril. Before we were married, we were living together in Boston. He had a big birthday coming up, so I planned a surprise party. Twenty-plus people had flown in from all over the world for him. He thought I was taking him to dinner as we walked up the Charles River to a dock where all his friends were hiding on a party boat. Success! No one in sight. Then they all jumped up and yelled, "Surprise!"

He turned to look at me with a big smile and quietly said, "You cunt!" and walked up the gangplank to greet his guests. Reeling, I had to figure out how to put on a brave face while questioning myself, deciding if I really heard him say that to me.

I still married him. *Yes. I'm an idiot.* This is my thought even today as I write this.

I'd met him while living in Tokyo, where he was stationed with the US military. I was living in serious isolation. It wasn't easy to meet people and make friends there. Needless to say, I was looking for some—any—connection. I met a group of very fun, active people in a running group. On the weekends, we went on some fun runs, and there he was. Funny. Popular. Smart. Accomplished. Had a growth path of his own. Self-driven. Big social circle. And the kind of guy everyone wanted to be around. Life of the party. Like really. The party was always in his apartment, even if he wasn't there.

With minimal observation, it would have been obvious that someone was always the butt of his humor, even then. And it certainly wasn't great when it was me, even if I could publicly and convincingly laugh it off, which is what I tried to do. Everyone on the receiving end tried to laugh it off. He was the life of the party, after all. It must have been funny.

Two weeks before our wedding, my mom—normally a soft touch—asked me a direct question.

"Are you sure you know what you're doing?"

"*Of course,* I do!" I answered. And I blew her off.

I ignored my mom's warning, but I never forgot that she asked the question. I mean, he wanted me. Why wouldn't I want him? I could fix things later. I was strong, right?

My marriage was short-lived but impactful. We moved to Europe with his US military job. More isolation. Every morning, I'd wake up and wonder what I'd done wrong the night before. I'd lay there cringing, waiting for the hammer to drop. Replaying the day before repeatedly, questioning what it would possibly be.

He'd yell about how I was too social, not social enough, paid too much attention to him, didn't pay enough attention to him, talked with someone too much, or didn't look right. Apparently, sometimes, I even intentionally sabotaged him. I had too many opinions and not the right opinions. I drank too much or not enough. I was too much fun. Or mostly, I was not enough fun. I wasn't good enough. It didn't matter how. It was always something.

The yelling. The isolating. The isolation. The conversations with others where he would directly and publicly assert that my opinion didn't matter. How could I know anything about anything? He was good at emphasizing my dependency. Being labeled a dependent as a military spouse played to his hand. Then one day, my husband put his hand or foot (I don't remember which) through the door rather than my face. I needed help, so I turned to the infrastructure on the base, trying to get out. It became clear that being a dependent in that system meant that I wasn't to be taken seriously. Not then. Not there. And it backfired on me because they told him I'd reached out for help.

I had to build a life for myself away from him. I left (actually, I considered it *escaping*) one day after he went to work. I didn't sleep well for months after that. When I did sleep, I had this recurring dream of him finding me, being in my house, and telling me he could get in because he had "a key to everywhere."

I wouldn't call my ex-husband a psychopath; I'd call him a domineering narcissist. He was a bully and very cruel when it suited him. He loved being the center of attention. He *had* to be. That meant he needed to dominate the conversation, the room, his relationships—everything. If you threatened his power and control or showed up in a way that he thought compromised him, then he'd "put you in your place." Directly. Publicly. Through jokes.

He dismissed and diminished me and beat me down until I was a shell of myself. I left our old friends behind. In my mind, they were his. And in many cases, that proved to be true. The breakdown of our marriage had to be my fault, not his, right? He was the life of the party.

Typically, no one knows what goes on behind closed doors with Lord At-Your-Peril. He thrives on power and control. Outsiders only see what he wants them to see.

 You write about two different guys—a boyfriend and a husband—but for you, they're in the same category. What was that like? Were you scared of those guys?

 Simple answer: Yes. In different ways. They were two completely different situations. The guy I married broke my spirit. It started way before we got married. And over time, he just broke me. In the end, I felt like I was a shell of myself.

It's a silly example, but it took a long time for me to be able to go out with friends at night and then wake up the next morning without this angst, waiting for the barrage of abuse that would come at me for whatever I did wrong the night before. Literally, it took years not to have that anxiety, which is crazy. With the boyfriend, it was more of a base fear, like the hair standing up on your neck, you know something bad is going to happen.

When you say broke you, do you mean emotionally? Physically? That's such a hard word, and it makes me so sad because I know you. I love you, and to hear that anybody would do that, I don't like it.

It's shocking to say that about myself. And at the same time, I believe I've always been a strong, independent, opinionated, of-my-own-mind person. But I allowed it! I'm ashamed. The fact that I allowed somebody to do that to me still brings me to tears.

With abuse, it starts with, "You're stupid," and, "Your opinions don't matter." Over time, it starts to break you down. I've read a lot of stories and research about abuse, and it all says that it's not my fault and blah, blah, blah. Okay, fine, whatever. But I was still a party to it. And that part hurts.

What's so ironic is that both these guys were attracted to me because I was determined and independent. But at the same time, they were threatened by that. In a lot of ways, they were turned on by their own drive to exert power and control over my strength and independence. Like if they could dominate me, a strong person, that said even more about them.

My ex-husband was all about power and control. If his power and control over me, over a situation, over a room, or over a party was threatened, he found ways to bring it back to him. He always found a way. In public, it manifested as him being the life of the party. He was the guy who was funny, who had stories. He would physically stand in the middle of a room and draw everyone's attention if that's what it took. And the stories. The jokes. Somebody in that room was always on the receiving end of whatever he was dishing out.

When I finally decided I needed to get out, I was living overseas and was a military dependent. I was all by myself and didn't have any help. I'd just found a new job and was starting to find strength from that. But right before I decided to leave, the abuse escalated. That's when I knew I had to move. That's when I became concerned for my physical safety. If he were to grab or push me, I could have explained that away. I could dismiss that. Like, *Oh, that wasn't as bad as I remember.* But when you have a hole in a wall or a door, it's right there in front of you.

It's important to be able to identify the patterns of a Lord At-Your-Peril, so you can get out of the situation long before you can't sleep or are staring at a hole in your wall. In trying to understand how I got myself into this abusive situation, I did a ton of research. I'm visual, so I gravitated to diagrams like those on the National Center on Domestic and Sexual Violence website (http:// www.ncdsv.org/publications_wheel.html). There are many abuse diagrams out there. They all effectively explain the boiling frog effect. The stages of abuse start out seemingly benign and inconsequential, and then the temperature gradually goes up. And you stay because you're normalized to the new state.

Name Calling

Power Games

Inappropriate Restrictions

Overprotection

Emotional Unkindness

Violation of Trust

Symbolic Aggression

Sexual Abuse

Cycle of Violence

Physical Violence

Domestic Slavery

Weaponization of Money

Weaponization of Children/Family

Degradation

Dismissal and Blame

Isolation

Mind Games

Cycle of Abuse Diagram: The inspiration
for this diagram came from dozens of places.

I love the diagram you included. I'd heard about these stages. I can see some of that very early stuff in my experiences, but it has never escalated past those early stages for me.

Yes. Well, the point is to see the signs and get out of the relationship, right? So, it's good you only know the early stuff. But if you don't get out of it, things are going to escalate with this Lord.

I got into the second situation with a charming sociopath. I was afraid of him because he was more physically unpredictable. We lived on an upper floor of a midrise building, and I worried—more than once—that one of us would go over the handrail on the balcony.

 If our readers could see me, I just had to take off my glasses and process that. Jeez almighty.

There was a lot of high energy going on in that relationship.

 Yes. There were big, blaring signs all over the place. Absolutely. And I didn't pay attention to them. I've thought a lot about this, as you can imagine. I grew up in a world where people were who they said they were, and I love that. But it also made me naïve. I never knew people could be like that, so I didn't know how to respond. And I dismissed *all* the warning signs. Lords At-Your-Peril are never what they seem to be.

 Didn't you have a strong core group of girlfriends or family you could call or talk to about this? Or were you trying to figure it out by yourself?

I have amazing people in my life—and all over the world—because I've lived all over the world. But when I got involved with both of these men, I was in a place of physical isolation, away from all those people. Of course, there were phones, but I was in a new place and was completely isolated. And I met both of these guys through people or situations that I trusted. They just didn't know this side of them.

I now know that isolation is something that predators seek out. And these guys are predators. They find your weak spots, and they exploit them. Being already physically isolated is a plus for them. And if you aren't already isolated, they will make you so. This is a fact. They will make sure that they are the center of your world. And maybe your whole world.

My Lord At-Your-Peril

I think my story is a case of early-onset Lord At-Your-Peril in many ways. I was walking in a sort of love fog with my guy, and no good could come of it. Early one Saturday afternoon, one of my best friends called me about Fishtank Boo (he used to build custom tanks for celebrities and athletes) and said, "Every time you call me or text me when you're with him, you're at a bar, a party, and drinking. Do you realize this is not like you? You barely drink, and now, you're day drinking and tipsy when the two of you are together. Be careful."

When a trusted girlfriend who has your best interest at heart offers up a warning, you need to listen. In this case, it wasn't easy for her to do that. After all, she'd introduced me to Fishtank Boo and loved us both. But a new, potentially destructive pattern was emerging, and at the time, only she could see it.

Thank God she shared it, and thank God I listened! She was right. This was not how I rolled. I was a social drinker only, and even then, I have a two-drink limit. It's just not my thing. But it was *his* thing, and it quickly became *our* thing. I loved this guy, but I woke up when I realized that I was sliding down the slope with him. We didn't end our relationship over this, but I self-corrected and found my way out of the fog.

He had introduced a habit—a pattern of behavior—that I'd never participated in before, and I was susceptible to it. But in order to date him, we had to be on 10 all the time. We pushed our relationship to the limits in every area: socially, sexually and emotionally. I was dating a functioning alcoholic and an adrenaline junkie. It was him, me, and whatever cocktail could get us there the fastest.

I'm not sure if he realized at the time that he had a problem. He knows now. In fact, he's been sober for almost two years. He was in a near-fatal motorcycle accident after he was out drinking which was his catalyst for change.

If I go back to the abuse diagram, we were on the outer ring. We were building our relationship on addiction. I don't know what would have happened if we stayed together, but ultimately, nothing good could come from it.

So, it's nice to have people around you who know who you are and can see things you can't see, so they can flag it when patterns change. I might've been able to catch that myself, but I didn't think about it. I think a general lesson is to get a handle on who you are so that when you enter into a relationship, you are firmly anchored in your own self and don't move according to who you bring into your life.

You, thankfully, took the warnings to heart, and that's the healthy thing to do. You were smart. You paid attention. You knew yourself. Even if you had to be reminded. Sounds easy and obvious. But it's not an easy thing to do.

About those early warnings: Don't dismiss them. Silly example: it's not okay for somebody to call you "Dumb" or "Stupid." Those are not terms of endearment. It's not okay for someone who supposedly loves you to tell you that your opinions don't matter. That's not someone you need to be with. It's that simple. And I just got chills because I'm so ashamed that I didn't heed those warnings myself. There were a thousand of them, and I should've paid attention.

If you find yourself making excuses for them and you say things like, "Oh, that was just a one-time thing," or, "That couldn't be as bad as I remember," please walk away. And then you never have to deal with the guys I dealt with or worse—because there's a lot worse. I mean, my case was nothing at all compared to some other stories.

 Do you think that one or both of yours could have been headed down into those unspeakable wells of physical abuse or death?

 No doubt. It's so important to take a look at the abuse diagrams because all those circles before you get to physical abuse are equally important. When you leave someone during these early stages, people don't usually think things were that bad. It's easy for people to dismiss you as being dramatic. In my case, I walked away without broken bones or physical signs, but with both men, it was a perilous situation for very different reasons. But I dove far enough into these circles that I finally woke up to the signs. Then when I started looking back, it was like, "Oh shit. What was I thinking?"

Lessons Learned from Lord At-Your-Peril

- Lord At-Your-Peril is a predator. This Lord is manipulative. Lord At-Your-Peril is even charming and certainly doesn't seem crazy at first meeting. This Lord is the absolute opposite of that.
- Believing that people are who they say they are can make you more vulnerable to this Lord.
- Lord At-Your-Peril can show up in many forms. Remember the diagram of abuse.
- Pay attention to shifts in patterns, be open to loving feedback, and respond accordingly with friends.
- Don't ignore the red flags. Don't dismiss the seemingly small slights. Don't ignore the put-downs. They might feel like they are one-offs and are no big deal, but they are warning signs—signs to leave.

If you're already in a relationship with Lord At-Your-Peril, you are the only one who can get yourself out of it. And you are the only one who can put in the work to heal yourself once you do get out of it. But—big BUT—you are not alone. Begin by reaching out to someone. Anyone. Break the isolation. Get help.*

And what can you do if you have a friend or family member in an abusive relationship? You can be supportive, but you can't fix it for someone else. Help empower that person. Don't judge them. Encourage them to participate in things outside of their abusive relationship. Help them develop a safety plan. Encourage them to talk. You can't rescue them, but you can continue to show them that there's a different life outside of their abusive world. And you can be there for them when they start to rebuild themselves.

*There are a lot of resources out there you can draw upon, including the national domestic violence hotline at www.thehotline.org.

9

LORD GOOD GUY, NOT MY GUY

I was excited to go on a Valentine's Day date, and at the same time, I had an acute sense of dread. *Did he think this was the beginning of an exclusive relationship? Had I led him to think that's what I wanted?*

I had a secret. For at least a week, I knew that I was seeing a good guy, hell, a *great* guy, but not *my* guy.

good guy

noun

: a morally correct person or character: a hero

ord Good Guy, Not MY Guy is usually attentive, articulate, fun, honest, and educated. This Lord is generous in terms of time and pocketbook, and you always look forward to your dates together because this Lord is creative and plans dates with purpose. But as this Lord tries to pull you closer, you inch back. On the spectrum of humanity, Lord Good Guy, Not MY Guy is a damn fine person—good with kids, dogs, the elderly, and you. It's hard to find such a good guy.

So, why don't you want this Lord?

Meet Lord Good Guy, Not MY Guy. He's perfect in every respect, except for that one thing. Actually, two critically important things: *chemistry* and *timing*. It's just not there. Or it's kind of there and kind of not. And every time you see this Lord, deep down, you know this is not *your* guy.

A Valentine's Day date with me, Lady FOMO. Warning. Warning. We were three weeks into the discovery phase, and Valentine's Day was up next. My new guy made reservations at a notable restaurant with a James Beard award-winning chef. I was excited to go coupling on Valentine's Day, and at the same time, I had an acute sense of dread. Did he think this was the beginning of an exclusive relationship? Had I led him to think that's what I wanted?

I had a secret. For at least a week, I knew that I was seeing a good guy, hell, a *great* guy, but not *my* guy. Because we'd just started seeing each other, I hadn't fully discussed my open dating philosophy, and he was flying blind to who I was. As I danced around my personal elephant in the room, I moved further away emotionally while he was trying to draw me closer. I had to face the music and lay my cards on the table. Result—our relationship ended that day. We were not only on different pages; we were in different chapters.

The One

Okay, let's dig a little deeper and talk frankly about the One, the shiny object most singles who are actively in the dating scene are chasing: the good guy. And depending on who's talking, there are three distinct approaches to catching this prize.

- **The Wait and See Approach**: "If you would just stop looking so hard, the One will show up."
- **The Divine Intervention Approach**: "God is preparing that Special One just for you. All you have to do is get prepared for him."
- **The Catch and Kill Approach**: "Honey, you need to get out there. You aren't going to catch the One sitting on your couch watching Netflix. Get out and go hunting!"

Ring a bell? Doesn't it feel like we're on a constant dating safari, perched on the back of our jeeps, binoculars tightly pressed against our faces, intently looking for the One? Because in our minds, good guys can seem rare and endangered. Everyone is after them, and when one is caught, the world has one less eligible person to hunt.

The truth is: that's not true. Not at all. There are a lot of good guys out there, with more joining the ranks every day. And here's the shocker: most of them aren't going to be *your* guy. Most of them will prove to be Lord Good Guy, Not MY Guy. It's all about compatibility, timing, desires, needs, expectations, and making all of those things map together.

The problem with having a catch and kill mentality is that when you find a good guy in the wild, so to speak, you get so wrapped up in the capture that you forget to ask, "Is he *my* guy?" And the only way to know that is to know yourself. When you know what you want in life, even a little bit, you can better judge your long-term compatibility and know if he's the right guy to date in your particular season.

So, how can you tell? Ladies, if you're really in tune with what you want and what you need, you should be able to measure compatibility and chemistry pretty quickly. So, sit down, and think about your basic deal-breakers. Then, think about your wants, the partner you want, and get specific and honest with yourself. Write it all down and tell your friends about *your* guy. Get serious about visualizing this person, so much so that you can see them and hear the conversations you'll have when you're enjoying time together. Then, when you meet someone who meets your paper standards, you can better determine if they are worth the investment. The question "Could they be the One?" becomes easier to answer.

A good guy checks all your boxes. He brings the basics to the table. The question is, can he *really* bring it—whatever "it" means—to you? Can he bring the passion, the ambition, the juice to the relationship? If so, then you might be on the right track. Checking the boxes is a good start, but does he have the flavor you're looking for? Bottom line, do you two have *chemistry?*

One of the questions I ask myself when I'm dating a good guy is, "Can I imagine taking my clothes off in front of him?" If the answer is "Eh, not really," then *this is not my guy*! I think we all should have a question like this tucked away to help us find our way.

And timing is definitely important. You can meet a great guy today and either not see him (meaning you pay him no notice), or you date him and determine he's not your guy. Then you bump into him a year later, and everything changes. Seasons of life and timing are important.

 Here's the deal. My Lord Good Guy, Not MY Guy in the opening story, was recently divorced and was trying to decide how to navigate the dating world. I was ten years past my divorce and loving my newfound rhythm of open dating. We were in different seasons, but we gave it a whirl anyway because we liked each other and had obvious chemistry.

What I learned was that he was wicked creative, thoughtful, and patient, which meant that at various times over the course of three weeks, I was the recipient of lovely gifts and gestures. Upon my return from an international trip, he brought me dinner and gave me a handcrafted card with beautiful wildflowers as a "thinking of you" gift. He even customized a Spotify playlist. His efforts weren't overbearing; he was being true to his expression.

Many of you might be thinking, *Girl, he sounds like a great guy! He could be the One. What's your problem?* Fair enough. The problem was that I couldn't separate his kind gestures from the implied hopes and expectations that they seemed wrapped in. I was seeing other people, and I felt like he was trying to lock me in. Our different seasons were too far apart. He was Hot Summer, and I was Cool Winter—both beautiful and restorative but not within reach of one another. So, I had to resolve that this *great guy* was just not *my guy*!

I have a few stories with Lord Good Guy, Not MY Guy too. But while we got to know each other well enough for me to know he was a good guy, it was also plenty of time to know that he wasn't my guy. I could tell pretty quickly.

I dated one of them for a short while. He was physically my type: tall, dark, and handsome, of course. Smart. Accomplished. He'd taken up a martial art form just before we met. He was good at it, quickly. He had aptitude for whatever he did. He was a doer and great conversationalist too. He took me to nicer places than I would indulge in on my own. At some point, he made the move, but I just couldn't get there. I knew it way before I acknowledged it.

He was such a good guy. I just kept questioning myself about why he couldn't be *my* guy. Why couldn't I make that work? Maybe if I'd said something sooner, we could have salvaged a friendship. But I waited too long. He wanted too much and then thought I hadn't been truthful. It's hard to feel okay when you're on the wrong end of the "it's not you, it's me" conversation. I ended up hurting him.

There are a lot of good guys around. But can you identify which ones aren't *your* guy?

Wow. That is the question! I think it's been different for me each time.

There are a lot of men out there who are wonderful and single and are looking for love and relationships. We ignore them because of whatever list we've created in our mind or our seasons of time. If you're really not in the season of being in a relationship, you may pass ten good guys in a week and never see them because you aren't open to it.

When I dated my Lord Good Guy, Not MY Guy, it was purely a matter of timing, and maybe a few other things, but mostly timing in that case. And it just wasn't going to work.

 I totally agree. There are a ton of good guys out there, but for the good guy to be *your* guy, the stars must align. Timing is so important. Like in my example, timing was part of it, for sure. But the additional piece that we haven't mentioned much yet is *chemistry*. There has to be chemistry for more than a friendship, and it wasn't there. And you can't quantify chemistry for somebody.

I have girlfriends who pass on a guy saying, "Oh, I don't feel it."

And then I remind them, "Well, you're looking at a guy from across the room. You can't know if you feel it or not. You haven't even talked to him."

Some good guy might walk past you, but if he doesn't have the right hair color or whatever, you're not open to him. You won't even consider him because you think, *Oh, I'm not dating him because he doesn't look right.* So, you don't even know if he's a good guy, or maybe your guy, because you're not even open to talking to any guys who aren't a perfect insta-fit. And then you say that there are no good guys.

So, you have to be open to a guy, open to dating. Otherwise, how do you know if there is or isn't chemistry? In my case, I was open to it and was asking myself, "Why can't I feel it? Why can't I get there?" The chemistry simply wasn't there. But you have to be open to even get that far.

Chemistry. Yes. Hell yes! A lot of it is chemistry. Actually, *most* of it is chemistry for me. And there's a battle raging when you say, "Why can't I make this work? Is it me? How can I make this work?" The conflict is that you kind of like this guy, and he could be the one. And at the same time, you're battling this lack of chemistry, trying to make them match.

You're trying to force fit it. You talk yourself into it.

Therein lies that moment when you have to decide and act. Even though you know he's not your guy, you have to face the music and toss him back. You have to choose to keep looking and add more time to your timeline. This step is a difficult but critical one that will lead you to the right guy. *Your* guy.

That reminds me, I've heard you mention that some good guys you know said that women don't want good guys; they want bad boys.

That's it. The bad boy thing. Well, I've been that woman. I probably still am a tiny, tiny bit. I love that type. I love the rebel. I love the guy who operates on margins, who's not afraid to . . . Well, there's a whole list of reasons why I think those guys are sexy, but what about you? You've done this, right? Where you're like, "Ah, he's a little too vanilla." Boring. Predictable. Right? You're like, "Come on, man, can I just live a little before I settle for that?"

Yes, and you can't go there if that isn't what you want.

I actually feel bad for the guy that's been properly raised, is respectful to women, holds down a good job, doesn't swear like a sailor and has some good at-home training. They can get outshined by the guy who lives life with reckless abandon and doesn't give two f#@ks about what other people think. Listen, he might be your walk on the wild side, but you better hope your ass isn't in jail by the end of the week!

I hear you. But these good guys feel this way because they're chasing after women like us. They don't chase after women who want what they want.

Excellent point. Way to put it in perspective. It's true. And one example, I won't say which of my men it was, but it's one I was married to. After we got divorced, I said he should consider dating a woman who he used to go to church with, "She's perfect for you. She's dah, dah, dah, dah." All the things. And he was like, "I don't want her."

See? Good guys want bad girls. Maybe we're all doomed!

I wish I'd walked away from the assholes I dated as quickly as I walked away from the good guys. I struggled to find examples of good guys for my story because I didn't date them long enough to have anything interesting to say. All my stories are about assholes.

Wow. Do we wish we'd walked away from the assholes in our lives sooner than we did the good guys? And why didn't we? Is it because we both like a little bit of that bad-boy syndrome?

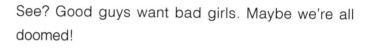

I don't know, but I do know that we're both competitive. There's a bit of a thrill to competition, and I think that the guys we walked away from more quickly didn't give us that.

Yeah, it was too easy. I want to feel like I won. I want to come out feeling like I won something.

Lessons Learned from Lord Good Guy, Not MY Guy

- Know yourself and what you want. Experiment with your wants and desires and see how compatible you are. Ask questions, ask questions, ask questions.
- Define what a good guy means to you. How can you tell if he's not the one?
- Don't be afraid to throw a fish back in the pond or release a tiger back into the wild. If he's not *your* guy, let him go! Even if you have insecurities around aging, the desire to have children, angst over finances, etc., don't settle.
- There are a lot of these good guys out there. A select few are going to be *your* good guy.

10

LORD MY GUY

It was intended to be an hour, max. When we left the bar seventy minutes later, he kissed me on the cheek, and we went our separate ways. But not before I looked back, and he saw me look back. How cliché. But it was joy.

Lord My Guy will be unique to you—obviously. But in general, there are some common traits that play into finding him and/ or knowing if he's, wait for it, "the One." Below are some signs that you're right for each other right now.

Timing is right: The two of you are in the same time frame or season of life, meaning you have the same or similar relationship intentions at the same time. You're both available for each other at the same time. Timing is huge!

It's easy: When you meet Lord My Guy, things will be easy. We don't mean everything comes together perfectly. No way. No how. Every day is a journey. We do mean that you won't find yourself trying to force-fit yourselves into situations and activities that aren't you. You won't be making excuses to yourself. You won't be trying to justify anything. You can simply be you. You'll accept him for who he is too. Just think of all the time and energy you'll have on your hands without all the added second-guessing and trying to be somebody you aren't. Whew!

You complement, rather than compete: If you've found Lord My Guy, you won't be on the treadmill competing for his affection. Your insecurities will be lower, and your honesty and vulnerability will be raised.

Here's a telltale sign. If you're spending a lot of time trying to be the perfect version of yourself in order to keep or please your guy, then you're being driven by the fear of losing him. You're probably competing with the shadow of someone else who may steal his attention. On the flip side, if you're thinking about how to positively add to your relationship, content with who you are and what you bring to the table, then you're creating a habit of being a complement to your partner. Good job. That will pay off; we promise.

You'll have a "good beginnings" story: Sounds strange, right? Yes, but it's also foundational. Shouldn't everyone have a good relationship beginnings story? Hopefully. It's not foolproof, but it's symbolic of compatibility and, yes, timing. It's one of those questions you will always hear: "So, how did you meet?" It's inevitable, and you'll be asked frequently. If this is a good and fun story to tell, it adds that much more to your relationship.

We met at a wine bar. I had an unwritten rule of not staying longer than an hour for any first blind date. Yes. I said *blind date*.

When I walked in, I saw this beautiful man across the bar turn toward me and look me in the eye. I thought, *Okay, let's hope that's him.* It was. We got seated, and I proceeded to be very specific—uh, maybe picky—with my wine order. I asked lots of questions. Seriously, I sounded high maintenance, even to myself.

We had a great conversation. Time flew. When we left the bar seventy minutes later, he kissed me on the cheek, and we went our separate ways. But not before I looked back, and he saw me look back. How cliché. But it was joy.

He waited all the way until 7:00 the next morning to ask me out again.

David is my Lord My Guy.

Did I mention that we didn't get pictures, places of work, or last names before we met? He was described to me as a health nut. It's no small thing to be called a health nut living in San Francisco. I was worried. I mean, I eat fairly healthy, but I eat whatever I want, whenever I want. I work out because I love it. I'm not a regimented person. When I hear health nut, I hear the proselytizing vegan whose way is the only way. David was not that. He's definitely a practicing carnivore and a gym rat, yes. Based on the pre-qual we had on each other and our first meeting, it was pretty quickly decided all the needs were met. Then it was on to discovering whether the wants could be satisfied. The fun part.

He called me right away. We've never been into game playing. Such a relief. On that first call, he asked me out for Sunday evening. We went to dinner then a jazz club. Conversation was easy and fun and intoxicating. I don't remember anyone else even being in the room at either place, which is not an exaggeration because, at some point at the jazz club, David and I got a surprise when the host asked us to move to the back of the club because we weren't showing the proper amount of interest (meaning none) in the artists.

The very next day, I called and asked if I could have ninety minutes of his time on Wednesday.

"Sure," he said.

He was going to be joining the board of the San Francisco Zoo and had never even been there, so I whisked him off to the zoo for his birthday lunch just one week after we met the first time. Despite getting rained on, it was a quick burst of random fun. The best part: He was totally okay just going with it, not knowing where we were going or what we were going to be doing. He was all in.

I sort of got to meet David's mom that afternoon. She called on our way back to his office to let him know that she'd moved back to her home that he and his sister had moved her out of years prior. She figured out a way to buy back her home without anyone else knowing, and she lived six hours away from that home. How could I not fall in love with this woman instantly? She knew what she wanted. She went and got it. Then informed others when and as needed. David's reaction was precious. I mean, what can you do, really? But he talked her through it, tried to understand if she was safe, had a laugh, and told her he'd see her soon.

David met all my local friends within the next week at a birthday party, a trivia night at a bar. It was Bible trivia shipped in by one of our friends in the South to test the birthday boy. David ended up winning. "Who is that guy? He needs to be on my team!" "You recruited a ringer! How'd you know it was Bible trivia?" I couldn't have planned it better. Turns out David hails from generations of Methodist ministers. It's in his genes, and he sat in church every Sunday. All good fun. So much laughing.

"You're going to think I'm crazy, but I have a trip planned to Mexico next week. Want to go?" he asked. I responded, "Uh, you're going to think *I'm* crazy, but yes." I was on a business trip in Minnesota. So, I had to meet him in Cabo after he'd already been there a day. He was waiting for me at the airport. In person. (Seriously big points!) We made out in the taxi the whole way to the hotel, like get-a-room, embarrassingly so. Poor driver.

Within a few months, we moved in with each other. A few months after that, we were engaged. We eloped after knowing each other for ten months. Everyone thought we were on a snowmobile trip in Yellowstone. Over the course of secretly planning our Mexico wedding, we had six weeks of paperwork and questioning and conversations about each of our histories. It was gathering divorce certificates, death certificates, birth certificates, and seeing all the information on all these documents. We talked to each other about it, answered all the questions the information raised, and finished what needed to be completed on the forms to take those next steps in Mexico. It was a getting to know you phase like you don't normally think about. There was no hiding. No apologizing. No feeling like there needed to be a certain spin put on some little or big fact. No drama. It was enlightening and grounding.

About that time, I took him to my financial planner. Full disclosure, right? When we left, David asked if I was going to be okay moving my investments. What? Short story: there are some compliance rules with David's job. My planner knew it. I was the only one who was surprised. I didn't know what I didn't know, but it wasn't a problem. We were rolling with each other's strengths. And, David is better at money than I am, for sure. It's his world.

We do think differently about some of the tactics. I'd never bought a lottery ticket in my life. It didn't seem responsible to me. David, on the other hand, has fun with them. He calls them our "high-risk investment strategy." At the end of the day, we both work hard, we're both incredibly responsible, and neither of us feels the need or even the desire to chime in on anything the other might purchase.

It was quickly obvious that we move the same way. We encourage each other the same way. Go? Do? Grow? Challenge? Compete? Yes. We have so many examples.

"A marathon is on your bucket list? Which one do you want to do? I'll train with you."

"Uh, I just went big on a stock buy."

"Oh. That's why you're not sleeping? You believe in the move?"

"Yep."

"What's the worst that can happen?"

"We lose the house, and the dog decides to move in with the new owners."

"I see. I don't think we can live without the dog."

"A recruiter called me to find out if I know someone for this job in North Carolina."

"Really? Tell me more. That sounds great. You should ask about it for you!"

"I have an opportunity to do some coaching for this dynamic company. I'm uncertain because it's out of state, and I'll need to be on-site months at a time."

"You should do it. How can I help make it work for you?"

These are the conversations we have all the time about things big and small.

We come from different worlds, but we're grounded in many of the same things. David is in the world of finance. I've moved from consulting to founding and running a men's apparel business. We're both coaches and advisors, both formally and informally. We're both into continuous learning. He prefers more formal coursework and degree programs. I prefer experiential learning, masterclasses, and jumping right in. We're both avid—maybe insatiable—readers. He writes in and highlights his books. So, if I want to read one of his books, he knows to give it to me first. We both have incredible tolerances. And similarly, our tolerances haven't always served us well. We're both at the point where if something doesn't make us happy, there better be a really, really good reason to continue whatever it is. We're both direct, so we understand that in each other. We're honest and authentic with each other, even if we have to say, "That's something I don't want to talk about right now." We have learned to use our words with each other in a way we never could in past relationships.

We're both morning people. But he is a breakfast person. And a lunch person. I'm a coffee until about 10:30-ish person. Maybe lunch if I remember. Dinner is family time and often friend time, and it's important to me. We learn to navigate all of these things as we go. It's a journey.

The important thing is that we know each other, we're getting to know each other, and we move with each other. Even as we still discover things about each other, it's like a learning moment and not some big shocking discovery that someone was holding back. We're open, and we go with the flow. Sometimes, with great success, and sometimes, we have to figure out how to flow differently. I'm his biggest fan. And he, mine. We need each other to be all we each want to be. We help each other get there. And, we also have an us that we work on. All the time.

The best part is that we laugh a lot.

 So, Terresa, you found your Lord My Guy.

Yes, I did, but I was looking. You're not looking for Lord My Guy, Jes. You're still having fun dating around.

That's true. But I have a lot of questions about this. I want to ask some personal things before we talk about the general Lord My Guy.

When you first met David, was it like, "Oh my gosh, this is my guy"? Were you pretty sure? You wrote about how you looked back, and he looked at you and all that stuff.

I know, it's so cliché, but it was true. He called me before 7:00 the next morning. So, that kind of says, "no games," right? He wanted to see me again. He wasn't worried about "Oh my God, I'm going to wait three days" to call her because that's what you're supposed to do blah, blah, blah. He was like, "I want to see her. I'm going to call her. We're going to set a date."

I can't say that's exactly when I knew, but it was nice. Like when I first saw him, we were across the bar from each other, and I said to myself, *I hope that's him.* It was comfortable. Not *boring* comfortable, I don't mean that. It was like, *Huh, this is what it's like when the Legos fit together.*

Timing was critical. I'd been back in the US for a while at that point, but I'd been globe-hopping and making a ton of dating mistakes, as you now know. And he was married at that same time and having kids. Our getting together was all about timing.

Then, he hired the same dating service I did because he didn't have time to go out and meet people himself. He was looking. He wanted to meet somebody. I think he had a lot of fun with the dating service, and he met a lot of people. Now, he says that I was the only one they introduced him to. Sweet, but not true.

 You're obviously meant to be with one another. One of the things that I admire about your relationship is that you respect each other a great deal, and you respect your professional careers. And as I look back at the other Lords, there always seemed to be a tinge of competition. Like the Lord had to win, or you and I felt like we had to win, and there was this competition all the time. But with Lord My Guy, it's about complementing each other and making each other better.

 Absolutely. David and I are both very competitive. We're extremely competitive! For example, if you challenged David to lose ten pounds first, and he only had ten days to do it, he would lose eleven pounds before ten days. He's super competitive. FYI, in that specific challenge, I would look at you and ask ,"Why?" and pick up my glass of wine.

But how it works for *us* is different. In fact, both of us told our dating agent, almost verbatim, "I need somebody who can keep up with me. And someone who can push me, who's not going to hold me back, who can keep up and will also push and help me grow, help me go farther." And I think you have to be competitive to do that. I also think you have to be confident to do that in a complementary way, right? Otherwise, it becomes this "I beat you, you loser," and that's not what we do at all. We're more like, "Hey, what's our next challenge? What's your next challenge? How can I help?"

I love that. That's so good. What's your advice for people who've read this book and are saying, "I resonate with all these Lords, and I just want to find Lord My Guy"?

It took margaritas after my birthday to get me to change my approach. I was out with some friends, and we were drinking margaritas out of pitchers with straws, not glasses. That's when I made the call to this dating service and left a message. I'm sure I sounded sober. Not! They were closed for the holiday period, but in my drunken brilliance, I thought, *If I really want to find somebody, I've got to do something different. And, clearly, I don't know how to do that for myself.* So, I called the dating agency. What did I have to lose? The funny thing is that I didn't remember that I'd called them. When they called me back ten days later, my sober self had to dig into my drunken self's memory to know what they were talking about. Oh boy!

So, maybe it's important to evaluate and audit how you've been moving. If you're not getting the results you want, then do something a little drastic or seemingly out of your norm. Just to see what happens.

For some people, out of the norm is being open to the guy who's asked them out or the guy in front of them. The guy they'd normally say no to.

You know, when I'm ready to move out of my serial dating space, I think the key for me will be to break my patterns. To not be a prisoner of my own open dating routines. Because if I don't, I'll end up carrying this serial dating framework into a new chapter, but a new chapter has different rules, right?

So, I think anybody who doesn't have a Lord My Guy yet needs to think about their former dating patterns. And then decide what it's going to take and what you need to do to move into that next phase.

Hmm. I wonder if that means that you're avoiding the guy who could be your Lord My Guy right now because you're not ready to do that?

I wouldn't be surprised. I'm sure I've probably met men who could've been Lord My Guy. Like you said, it's all about timing. To have the flexibility and freedom that I want right now means that I'm potentially missing a Lord My Guy along the way. I realize that.

But I think the way you've dated has put you ahead of the game because most people don't know how to date multiple people. A lot of people get stuck feeling some sort of weird obligation to only keep dating one person until it works or implodes.

I would say that the majority of women who date some-one once or twice aren't sure what that means for them. (More on that in the next chapter). Should she keep dating him? Does he expect her to be exclusive? They don't know what to do, which is where communication and being clear about what you want has to happen pretty fast.

There's no glossary of terms that are universally accepted. The lexicon is different. The language is different. So, when you have a bit of an unconventional approach to dating, all your definitions are usually weird. I have to actively help people understand my lexicon.

So, you talked about how easy it was with you and David. When you say it was *easy*, what does that mean in terms of the feeling and experience?

It was easy in the sense that I wasn't trying to talk myself into anything. Not trying to force-fit anything. I wasn't saying, *Well, maybe he meant this or that.* I wasn't trying to justify anything. It was smoother than that. I didn't have any red flags in my head. The pressure wasn't there. And I wasn't trying to *win.*

There are things that are subtle or unspoken within us that another person can address, maybe unknowingly, that make it easy for you. Outside of the phone calls and other external things, there's something spiritual about being with someone who's easy to be around. With somebody you don't have to wear a mask with because you can simply be yourself.

I think you can reflect on people you've dated in the past, and with the benefit of that hindsight, say, "Okay, I see where the friction was. I see where I was trying to force-fit things. I get where I was feeling some pressure or tension." And that means it wasn't right.

Especially around Lord Good Guy, Not MY Guy because everything should be working, and yet somehow, it doesn't feel easy because you're *trying* to make it work. Like when David called you before 7:00 a.m. You wanted to see him again, so that seven o'clock phone call was welcome. You were excited, and you were like, *Yes, he's on the same page as me; this is awesome! I'm so glad to hear from him.*

Absolutely. It's all about timing and knowing what you want. And when you've met Lord My Guy, he gets it from the beginning. Like I said, it's like two Legos that fit together. At last!

You've likely met Lord My Guy when:

- The timing works for both of you
- The relationship is easy
- You complement each other
- You have a good beginning
- You know

11

OH, LORDS! MY FRIENDS DON'T KNOW HOW TO DATE

It's a funny little word, *dating*. And it can create a bit of confusion. For instance, most people will tell you they're *dating* the person with whom they have an exclusive or committed relationship. Others will go on a date with a different guy every other weekend and tell you they are *dating*. Both are correct.

So, how do we interpret the term?

Remember Lord Layaway? He was the Lord who shopped around and put his ladies on layaway. He wasn't completely flawed in his strategy; in fact, he got it half right. The shopping part of his methodology was on point. That, my friends, is dating. Obviously, shopping (or dating, in this case) is the act of checking things out, looking around, trying someone on for size, figuring out what they are going to cost you (ha, ha—but seriously), deciding if they add value, and comparing them to other potential partners in the store.

You get the idea. Let's face it: When you're dating, you should be thinking about what works and what doesn't! Simple as that.

Buying, however, is the transaction. This is the moment where you say, *Ah ha, I think you're my person.* So, you bag 'em up and take 'em home. This is a groundbreaking moment because neither of you fit in the active dating category anymore. You're now in the exclusive, committed, partnered world where you continue to go on dates with each other and explore the possibilities of your dating relationship. For the time being or forever, you're out of the dating game.

Cool, now that we know what we're doing, where are we going? Suitable stores are everywhere!

Where to Meet the Lords

- Online dating sites
- Referrals—Tell your friends and family you're up for being set up. Why not?
- Your Local Faves—Look around at the places you love checking out, doing the things you love to do. *Bonus: This is where you're likely to meet someone who probably loves those things too.
- Special Events—The best time to grab your people and head out into new crowds is during festivals, sporting events, live music concerts, Comicon, or whatever floats your boat; just go. Do!
- Value and Heart-Centered Spaces—If you're a churchgoer, then church. If you have a soft spot for animals, then maybe it's the shelter or horse ranch for rehabilitating kiddos.
- Business gatherings

Your Lord My Guy is potentially everywhere. Give him a chance. Let him give you a chance.

So, how does it work? First of all, chill out! You aren't exchanging the nuclear codes here; you're meeting people. So, be open to that first. The first exchange can be the most awkward, but let the moment guide you.

Once you get your footing and you've passed "Go," then you're off to the races. You've likely exchanged text messages and social handles so you can keep the ball rollin' with fun questions (see our Questions to Ask section) and fabulous flirtation! This is the *only* way you will get to know what kind of Lord you're dealing with. These steps seem obvious, but a lot of women cut men out before they start playing the game.

Rinse and Repeat, or like many of us, just repeat.

So, Jes, you're the one actively dating. Where do you meet people? How do you meet people?

Let's see. When I first got out of my marriage, I was on the scene a lot. I was out at nightclubs or at a rooftop bar in Raleigh, which was adjacent to where I lived. I'd go out with a girlfriend, and we'd look amazing, and then hit the town and pop in between these little bars and whatever. And that's how I met a lot of the men I dated in my thirties.

That friend was my wing woman, no doubt about it. And we had rules. We would not leave each other and go home alone. We always had a strict rule about that. If we were going to see somebody we met, we would see him on a different day. But we had a clear beginning and a clear end. And that worked, 99 percent of the time.

I was going to say it sounds very disciplined, but it also sounds like there were exceptions to the rule.

There were one or two exceptions, but they were mutual exceptions, and we were all good. That was my early thirties experience mostly. As I got older, like my late thirties, many of the men that I dated, I met professionally. I met them at conventions or ran into them in the work that I was doing. I did get set up a couple of times, but very rarely.

Impactful meetings, apparently.

Ha, yeah, the setups were weird for me. Anyway, I started getting into the dating sites because I thought it could be fun to put a specific mile radius around it. Go to DC. Check out people in Charlotte. Or all the way to Atlanta. I was also at the point where I was dating openly, and I didn't want to see men I was involved with often. So yeah, I went from traditional out-on-the-town club dating to professional dating, to a few referrals, to online dating.

Club dating, bar dating—everybody's there to meet people. Do you think being there in person makes it a little easier to meet people? You just have to qualify them later.

Yes. Oh, man. I think that was the biggest pool ever for me. The problem was that I would go home with four or five numbers, and then I'd spend the whole week jockeying with them. The texting, the this, that, not remembering what they were about. It was like a second job, basically trying to get these guys off my back. The chase. That was the fun part. I didn't want to deal with them afterward.

In my opinion, the club scene was the least qualified pool.

What about the business networking, conferences, and work stuff? Work venues are not necessarily where you're going to meet somebody. So, how does that happen?

Professional spaces can be a good place to meet a potentially good match. You just have to know how to move in them. Obviously, you're not hitting the clubs; this is different. In professional spaces, you need to put different attributes forward in order to make your way into a conversation. Being a good conversationalist is helpful, but feeling your way through by being an expert listener might be more clutch.

Bottom line, conferences and networking events can be rich with potential Good Guys, and after the business of the day is over, you can spend a little time meeting some at happy hours, bars, and restaurants.

So, you've moved from the bar scene where there's zero qualification, except they somehow managed to get to the same bar you did, to a work situation where there's a lot of qualification already done, but you don't know if they're single and looking. And then you go to the dating sites you mentioned as the third place you meet people. People self-qualify in a different way on the dating sites, right?

It's the opposite of conference dating, right? In conference dating, you're live and in person. I'm standing next to you. I know you're six feet or taller. I know what you look like in real life, and not just the picture you posted. I know how you speak about an issue. I know what you care about. I know if you're rude. I get all of that. I just have to dig a little. My biggest job in these moments is to determine if you're single.

Dating sites are the opposite. You go in understanding that the men on the site are single (according to them), and you can read all about his views and height and worldview. But eventually, you'll have to go on a date to find out if it's true. The ole' "Trust but Verify" method. I don't know if one is better than the other. My personality is more aligned with the conference type or being out and meeting somebody in person.

I don't know if you planned it that way, but it worked out that you just described three amazingly different scenarios.

Ha, how 'bout that? Lived experience wins again.

Beware of feeling weirdly attached after the second or third date! If you feel this way, it's because of one of two possible scenarios. Either you found "the One" and can't believe how magical the connection is. Or—and more likely—you feel this way because you want to date other people and have fallen into a premature and unspoken "exclusive rights agreement." You feel stuck, even though you've never discussed being exclusive.

One of the things that we talked about, and maybe even the impetus for this chapter, was some of our girlfriends who go out on a date, or two, or three, and then all of a sudden, they're not dating anybody else. They have this kind of weird attachment to this person or don't know what the situation is, so they get stuck. And they feel like they have to play that out before anything else happens with anyone else.

I would say that's most women that I know. Most of my girlfriends get caught up in this vortex of confusion. And after date two—especially if they like the person—there becomes this tension of wanting to see them but not wanting to be exclusive.

When I was going out to clubs in my thirties, I kept my options open. Yes, I might have met somebody a few weeks before and grabbed coffee with them a couple of times. I may have really liked them, but eventually, I'd feel this tension. Like, am I allowed to go to this rooftop bar this weekend with my girlfriends and meet someone else? Or am I oddly locked into some kind of pre-proposal for the rest of my life? It's crazy, right? And I think that's normal. And I think there's going to be a moment, a crossroads, where you have to be clear about how you date.

That feeling of obligation, of feeling stuck, comes from somewhere. It's real.

If you feel that way, there's a reason. There's a lack of clarity. When you're clear about something, you can move right through it. But when it's muddy, you aren't sure how to get through it. But why is it muddy? What happened to make this moment for you? It's your job to share with your new interest what you need to get unstuck, even if it means jeopardizing future encounters. If you feel obligated to be in a fake, exclusive relationship where you're hiding and making up stories about where you are on a Friday night, you're setting yourself up for failure. It won't work. Just be honest.

In some cases, it's just muddy. There's nothing else to it. So, get over yourself and get over feeling like you can't see other people. That feeling is in your head because you don't know how to date more than one person at a time. And the other person doesn't think you're obligated to him, right? So, maybe there is no underlying issue.

Maybe. But I think that oftentimes, we pull out all the stops on our dates. We want to be the most charming. We want to say the right things. We want to lead a man on because it's fun. It's fun to take them on the journey with you and show them how amazing you are. And they come right along with you, validating all your moves with increased interest.

Then you get to a point where you've divulged and given him your best right up front. Now, maybe he's hooked. So, now what do I look like, running around seeing four or five different men and hooking them all? How do you undo this? How do you honestly say, "I'm open, and I want to date other people," when you made it seem like you were all-in on this guy?

You just described becoming Lady Layaway when you really want to be Lady FOMO.

Yes. That's it. So, you have this slippery slope. I used to do that. In the past, I didn't use my words. You know how they say to two-year-olds, "Use your words." I didn't use my words. And next thing you know, I was doggone Lady Layaway and feeling kind of bad because that's not how I would like to move. One day I thought, *You don't have to move that way. You can be honest.* And that's what I started doing because it became a whole lot easier. And men are much more appreciative of that.

And sometimes, you feel weirdly obligated because you got too physical too fast. And then you're like, *Well, God, I already went there, so . . .*

Yikes! And how does that jive with your values? Experiences like these help you decide how to date. You say, "Okay, I decided to have an intimate, physical relationship with this person. So, anybody else I see, I'm not going to do that," or you say, "I'm not going to do that with any of them." And you go in knowing that you have some boundaries. Or you're like, "I'm going to have a physical relationship with all of them." And you need to be clear that your risks go up at that point, and you need to be prepared for that.

We have to treat dating like anything else we do in our life. We're such conscious people around the food we put in our body, many of us, or where we decide to live, and who we want to work with. And we get so fussy and particular. But then, when it comes to dating, we don't have that same level of concern for ourselves or understand ourselves well enough. And it's high stakes because you're picking a partner. You're picking somebody to invest your time and potentially share your body with.

We'll research which air fryer to buy, and we'll spend a damn hour on that and a bunch of money on it, but when it comes to a guy, not so. Whoever picks us up at a bar or whoever we pick up, we're just like, "Cool." And then we go home and sleep with them and wonder why we feel bad about it. It's incongruent.

 If you don't invest the time, you'll spend a lot of money on therapy! When you set the table with your expectations, he knows the rules. He's dating a woman who knows what she wants. So, now it's his turn.

 Does he know that she's put him at that table? Is that clear to him? Or is that only in her mind right now?

 As soon as she verbalizes, "I'm dating for a relationship," or she says, "I'm enjoying dating and meeting new people," the table is set that the woman wants to be in a relationship, or in the second case, is seeing other people and not serious yet. That's clear, and he can decide if he gets up from the table or not.

 Unless he's Lord Layaway. And then he stays at the table, and he's like, "Sure. I'm playing this game with you. And with you. And with you. And with you."

Lord Layaway has five tables in different restaurants with his name on them.

I actually think it's harder for women to sit across the table and say, "I'm not dating you for a relationship right now. I'm dating to date. I just want to get to know you." In theory, this should be very easy to say: I. Want. To. Get. To. Know. You. Seven words.

Right. But it is harder to say that to one guy and, at the same time, to another guy. And maybe even another guy. Because a lot of women feel like they have to play one out before they play another one out.

A lot of my friends can't juggle multiple men and dates. And not because they're weaving lies but because they feel like they wouldn't know how to manage three or four conversations in three or four dates. I get all that.

Because I date out of market, I don't have the added pressure of "come over to my house" or the pop-in. My friends go to dinner with one and go to lunch earlier in the day with another. And then Sunday brunch with some other guy. I'm not doing that.

The key for me is that all of the men I date right now know that I'm not dating them exclusively. They know I date other people. Period. I tell them early on. Like the day I meet them. I don't wait because I figure if that's not their jam, they should move on. Otherwise, it's time on the phone, and texting, dinner, and then what? On date two, I'm like, "Oh, by the way, I'm seeing some guy in Phoenix." And he's like, "I'm not into that." Well, then we just wasted a perfectly good evening. I could have been home or out with someone else.

Ask Questions

It comes down to being able to say what you want. But you're also asking this person questions about what they want too. So, there are the getting-to-know-you questions. What does your family look like? Do you have kids? What do you like to do? Hobbies, etc. There's all that. Then there are the "What do you want out of life?" questions, the "What are your values?" questions. Some of those get deep. But they're important because relationships are all about compatibility. So, how fast can you ask these questions? And how do you ask them?

I don't know. It depends on the person you're involved with. My experience is that I don't ask a lot. Most men I've dated always initiate the questions. Then I reciprocate. It seems like men are armed with these tactical questions that they want to get out of the way.

When I signed up with the dating agent, there were two men, actually in the same week or maybe the same ten days, who had a list for me. Because it was a setup, they were already kind of prequalified, and we had all of the basic information about each other.

Both of these guys went down a list: "Do you want to get married? Do you want to have kids? How many kids do you want?

Where do you want to live?" It was ten questions. Boom, boom, boom, boom. Holy crap! I never saw either of them again. I left quickly.

It is a turnoff to go straight into your dream list, the little list we talked about earlier that sits on your nightstand. Don't do that. It's weird.

Yeah! There was no fun to it. No romance. No flirtation.

Things should unfold naturally. Like if your kiddo calls, then that's a great time to give more information about them. Now, with that said, there are a few questions that you have to get out of the way quickly. And one is about dating intention. I think another is about kids. Do you want to have children? I don't think that comes out on the first date or the second date, but you should figure out how to navigate some of those important questions. If you're in your thirties and are dating thirty-year-old men who are single, they probably still want to have kids.

And a lot of thirty-year-old women are like, "I've got a clock ticking, here."

Exactly. So, it's important to explore that quickly because you don't want to fall for somebody when you can't meet their expectations—or they yours. Both parties need to know what they're talking about.

Religion can be a big deal. Culture can be a big deal. These days, people are a little bit more flexible about those things. And if you are, then that's fine. But if you're not, you need to date accordingly.

I agree. It's almost like you need to know your deal-breakers. Know yourself well enough to say what's critical. If you feel like a core value is going to be a stressor, then you have to say, "He might be hot, but he's not going to be the one." Keep it moving.

You can have a lot of deal-breakers that aren't about those things, but date accordingly. I dated one guy who was of a certain culture, and he knew—*always* knew—he would settle down with someone from his culture. But I didn't know that. So, why is this guy dating me outside of that?

Because he's having a good time. And you've got to know that you're his good-time girlfriend.

Which can be fine. If you know that and agree.

We shouldn't be in our heads all the time. It's like we jump to the checkmate before we've even moved the first pawn. Or we move one pawn, and we're like, "Ooh, I'm in a good position."

You have to have fun. Dating can be such work. But I think the more fun you have with it, the more success-ful you can be with your ultimate intention.

Dating is often opportunistic. I think, especially when you're younger, it's like, "I don't have to think about it. I'm just going to go out and meet people. And one of these days, I'll fall in love with somebody."

And you get caught up in the euphoria at the end of the night; how wonderful it was. And that's the fun part of dating. It's so fun. You fall in love on the first night. And then he doesn't text you. And then he's the worst person in the world, right? But that's the beauty of dating. All those ebbs and flows of emotion. The surprises and the delights.

Oh, this makes me want to go on a date. It sounds fun!

Recap: Don't Get Stuck

- If there's more to the attachment, and you think you've found "the One," then have that conversation and confirm or deny it with the Lord in question. That should clear things up.

- Maybe you slept with your date and only feel comfortable with a one-at-a-time approach to sex. Great, so date others, but don't have sex with them. Or don't have sex with any of your dates until you've established some kind of mutual exclusivity.
- Maybe nothing happened that led you to believe you're attached to them. It's just a feeling you have. Okay, so get over yourself. Now, go Lord shopping for your next dates.
- Or maybe—and most likely—you've thrown out your best lines, said some personal things that brought you closer to your date, and maybe conveyed, "Hey, I want to date you and only you," vibes—but you didn't mean it. Going overboard in the first two dates to show how interested you are can be misleading and trap you in a role that you hadn't intended to play quite yet.

You Are In Control

Here's the thing: At the end of the day, *you're* in control; *you're* in the driver's seat, so design your dating experience! Have fun with it, say what you mean, and mean what you say so you're truly comfortable and clear with your date along the way.

If you want a relationship, date Lords who want a relationship, not Lord Layaway!

And if you want to date around and stay single, don't date a Lord who wants a relationship.

The logic continues—if you don't drink, don't date the drinker. If you want to settle with a Catholic, don't date the Baptist. And so on and so forth.

You'll find out about your Lord and your compatibility by asking and answering questions and sharing experiences and information. It's a journey. Even if your destination is an exclusive relationship, the journey is important. Enjoy it. And, as you date and get to know each other, if you find it's not working or if red flags pop up, or something's not right, then release them and move on. Listen, if you're shopping for sweaters and find yourself in the shoe department, you've taken a wrong turn. Either turn around or reevaluate your intent. Sweaters or shoes? Not the same. At all.

- There are no rules. Ten minutes or ten dates.
- Once you know it's not right in whatever way, move on.
- And when all else fails, abide by the Golden Rule to release your Lord.

12

WE HAVE QUESTIONS!

There's an art and a science to asking questions as you're getting to know someone. You want to ask all the big important questions up front, so you don't waste anyone's time. If you want six kids, it's important to date someone who goes along with that. But asking that question on a first date? That's the fastest way to get labeled "crazy" or worse.

So, there is an *art* and *science* to asking questions.

The art part is the hard part. It's all about timing and tone. Timing is everything, and mastering the art of conducting a delicate yet essential conversation is crucial. The best approach is to first think about how you'd want to be asked about certain things. How would you receive certain questions in certain situations and settings? Being direct yet thoughtful will go a long way.

The questions themselves are usually the easy part. Saying them out loud can sometimes feel difficult or scary. But, if it's important to you, *ask* the question! If you've thought about the timing and tone, it will be easier. To practice, call a close friend (preferably the same sex as the person you're dating, so you can get their per-spective) and run a few of your questions by them. If they're truly a friend, they'll give you real feedback.

We thought it would be helpful to share some of the questions we've asked along the way to determine which Lord we were work-ing with. You'll recognize that this is our unique list because some of them are too crazy to have made them up. Consider them thought starters, use them as is, or read them for your amusement. We bet that you'll want to know the answers like we do. And you'll start brainstorming your own list.

PERSONALITY

- Do you have anger issues?
- Do you have control issues?
- Do you scream/yell at people? When was the last time?
- Half full or half empty?
- Limits or challenges?
- How often do you smile?
- How often do you laugh?
- How would you describe yourself in a social setting (i.e., Christmas party, family gathering, or a party where we both know no one)?
- In general, when you walk into a room full of people you don't know, are you energized, or does your energy evaporate?

CHARACTER

- What would you tell your daughter about men? And your son about women?
- Can you remember a time when you witnessed someone being treated badly? Did you do anything about it? What?
- Is there ever a time when you wouldn't be honest with the person you're dating?
- What does your "try" look like?

DATING NORMS

- How do you feel about long-distance relationships? How would you maintain it?
- Have you been in an open relationship? Did all parties know?
- How do you feel about open relationships?
- If I say, "I can't see you tonight; I'm grabbing dinner with friends," what do you hear?
- Would you have any issues with driving seventeen hours one way for a long weekend?
- Are you willing to commit (perhaps in writing) to holidays in (Idaho)?

PERSONAL / PROFESSIONAL PASSIONS

- Do you set goals? What's the next one?
- What is your biggest obsession in life?
- What hobbies do you have, and who do you do them with?

FAMILY & FRIENDS

- How many close friends do you have?
- Do you call them or text them? How often?
- Regrets?
- Who's your favorite family member and why?

FINANCIAL INSIGHTS

- What was your biggest financial mistake?
- Do you believe in having a housekeeper?
- Do you live on a budget?

TRAVEL

- Do you have a passport?
- Have you used it? Discuss.
- Have you ever planned a trip for someone else? Who initiated it?
- Have you traveled on your own?
- Can you be a spontaneous traveler? Would it matter where you went?
- Do you travel with your friends?
- How comfortable are you with couples' vacations?

PETS

- Are you averse to dog hair?
- Do you have a problem with a dog having the run of the house?

- What if you came home and the dog had chewed on your favorite shoe? What's your reaction?
- What if the dog got in the trash and spread it out in the living room? What's your reaction?
- What if I'm sick and it's raining, and the dog needs a walk?
- How do you feel about cats?

FOR FUN

- What do you consider a fun night?
- What about thong undies for men?
- Do you like to garden? What's your favorite crop?
- Do you put the seat down?
- Can you change a tire?

Write your own questions here:

_____

_____

_____

_____

_____

Listen, the dating world should be fun and fulfilling, but if it's not, start over. Try something new. Ask questions. Enter it lightly. Go for what you want. And don't be afraid to shop around!

There are a lot of people swimming in the singles' pool, and many of them want the same things as you. So, be clear about what you want, communicate it unapologetically, and go after it. It's all in your control.

ACKNOWLEDGMENT

A big thank you to super talented fashion illustrator Kristine Steiner for her collaboration on this book. You can find her on Instagram @kyjsteiner

ABOUT THE AUTHORS

Jes Averhart: I'm a Midwestern girl! I'm also a fourth-generation entrepreneur, creator of 28 Days of Reinvention and host of Reinvention Road Trip Podcast. I'm also the mom of a six-foot, five-inch teenage boy and one-foot, eleven-inch bulldog named Roscoe. Over the last two decades, I've worked with a portfolio of Fortune 500 companies and public sector organizations on the principles of transformational leadership, self-discovery, and the art of reinvention.

I realized my true passion for leadership development and women's empowerment while leading partner engagement at the *American Underground*, a *Google for Startups* Tech Hub (aka, the "Startup Capital of the South" by CNBC). After spending much of my time immersed in the startup scene, I was inspired to co-found *Black Wall Street Homecoming*, a nonprofit aimed at closing the funding gap for Black and brown tech founders.

I love writing in the mountains and on the beaches of North Carolina, cheering on the Ohio State Buckeyes, and globe-trotting. But without question, my greatest gift is my son Tre, who helps keep all things in perspective!

Find me on LinkedIn and at www.jesaverhart.com and www. reinventionroadtrip.com

Terresa Zimmerman: Founder of Wood Underwear®, entrepreneur, advisor, mentor, challenge seeker. I've always considered myself a citizen of the world but always wanted to be from that small town where everyone knows your name. My career progression takes on that look.

I started my career on the global stage and claim my "MBA" from lived world experience. Based around the globe, I worked with the world's largest companies on their brand and strategy challenges at pivotal moments of change for them and in the world.

Going from big corporate to being, perhaps, the only female founder of a men's underwear brand was a massive pivot and one that gave me a light-bulb moment: I love Main Street. Multi-generational store owners, new store founders, all people who give life and color to our small cities and towns. They make the world go round. That's where I love spending my time and energy.

I advise founders, business owners, and teams. I'm training for another marathon and forever trying to improve my golf game. David and I are always on the lookout for our next great adventure. We currently live in Raleigh, North Carolina, and Richmond, Virginia, with our Aussies, Whizkey and Tequila.

Find me on LinkedIn and at www.woodunderwear.com

Join our community on:

 - www.ohlords.com

 - @oh_lords

 - @oh_lords_book

 - @Oh, Lords

CPSIA information can be obtained
at www.ICGtesting.com
Printed in the USA
FSHW021301011021
85182FS

9 781955 711036